BREAKING THE CODE

BREAKING THE CODE REVISED EDITION: UNDERSTANDING THE BOOK OF REVELATION

Breaking the Code Revised Edition

978-1-5018-8150-3
978-1-5018-8151-0 eBook

Breaking the Code: DVD

978-1-5018-8154-1

Breaking the Code: Leader Guide

978-1-5018-8152-7
978-1-5018-8153-4 eBook

For more information, visit www.abingdonpress.com.

BRUCE M. METZGER
REVISED AND UPDATED BY DAVID A. DESILVA

BREAKING THE CODE

UNDERSTANDING THE BOOK OF

REVELATION

Abingdon Press / Nashville

BREAKING THE CODE REVISED EDITION
Understanding the Book of Revelation

Copyright © 1993, 2019 by Abingdon Press
All rights reserved.

Library of Congress Cataloging-in-Publication data has been requested.

ISBN 978-1-5018-8150-3

19 20 21 22 23 24 25 26 27 28 — 10 9 8 7 6 5 4 3 2 1
MANUFACTURED IN THE UNITED STATES OF AMERICA

In memory of Isobel Mackay Metzger
(1918–2016)

CONTENTS

PREFACE
TO THE REVISED EDITION

The book that closes our New Testament canon is not itself a closed book. When John sent it to his congregations in first-century Roman Asia, it was his hope that Revelation would illumine their world, would help them see its landscape and its challenges more clearly in the light of the whole witness of Scripture and in the light of God's unique and fundamental claim upon the allegiance and obedience of all who live and move and have being. Revelation is not meant to be a book that obscures our sight, but one that lifts the veil from all that obscures the spiritual significance of—and the spiritual dangers in—the choices that we make and the entanglements we must navigate on a daily basis.

It has been twenty-five years since Professor Metzger wrote his reliable guide to listening to Revelation's message, and his volume has contributed a great deal to mainline Christians' renewed engagement with this often off-putting conclusion to our canon. I was raised Episcopalian and eventually ordained United Methodist, denominations in which one is likely to hear readings from Revelation only on All Saints' Day and possibly at funerals. I share Professor Metzger's desire to see more Christians from such traditions allow Revelation to exercise its full, formative impact on them and their vision for discipleship. It was a privilege, therefore, to have been invited to revise and update Professor Metzger's work and to add something from the fruits of my own career-long study of Revelation to what he has offered.

A number of advances have been made in our understanding of Revelation since Professor Metzger completed his work. We have learned more about the dynamics of the cult of the Roman emperors and about what motivated and what was at stake for a city in worshiping a political ruler as a divine benefactor. We have become more sensitive to the deleterious effects of imperialism and colonialism and, as a consequence, have seen a new dimension in Revelation as an example of resistance literature. We have reflected more on the public ideology—the propaganda—of Roman rule, and as a result we have seen how Revelation is a far more politically charged text than readers might once have suspected. We have explored more fully what apocalypses are and how they "work" to change the perceptions and motivations of their audiences. All of these advances have also helped pastor-theologians perceive new dimensions in how Revelation's word challenges us to "keep the commandments of God and hold the testimony of Jesus" (12:17) across a broader spectrum of our life experiences. It is my hope that this revised and updated version of Professor Metzger's work benefits from these advances without losing any of his essential insights into the book and into our engagement with the world as faithful disciples.

While individual study will always be rewarding, Revelation is a text that is perhaps best heard and studied in community. It was written and first read to gathered assemblies in the context of worship and prayer; its word was conceived of as "what the Spirit is saying to the churches," and not to lone disciples. Its challenge is most fully and readily met by groups of disciples working together to discover and embody its word, and its ultimate goal is to call into being a new way of being human together before God. I would encourage you, if at all possible, to seek out other Christ-followers from your church, family, or circles to engage this study together.

David A. deSilva
Ashland Theological Seminary
Ashland, Ohio

PREFACE
TO THE FIRST EDITION

For most church members, the Book of Revelation is a closed book. They avoid it, thinking it too mysterious for them to understand. On the other hand, a few people seem to live in the Book of Revelation, concentrating all their reading of Scripture on this one book alone. Both of these extremes are shortsighted and ill-advised.

The Book of Revelation contains passages of great beauty and comfort that have sustained Christian believers over the ages. Doubtless there are parts that seem to the casual reader to be bizarre and bewildering. But when one approaches the book recognizing that it belongs to a special type of literature (the apocalyptic type), then one can begin to appreciate the overall message of John, the theologian of Patmos. Of course, some parts will remain enigmatic, but on the whole the attentive reader will be surprised to find how much of the book makes sense.

For a good many years the present writer has had an academic as well as a personal interest in the Book of Revelation. The task of giving lectures on Revelation to theological students as well as presenting Bible studies of this book to church people in various congregations has required both a scholarly and a devotional consideration of this remarkable book.

The approach of the present volume has in mind the needs and interests of the general nontheological reader. Special attention is directed to the literary form and the spiritual message of Revelation. Endnotes are kept to a minimum, and the application is more than once directed to present-day realities of the Christian life.

Quotations of Scripture are made from the New Revised Standard Version of the Bible. In the exposition of the text occasional phrases have been adapted from the present writer's comments on Revelation in *The New Oxford Annotated Bible* (New York: Oxford University Press, 1991).

In conclusion, I must thank many who have contributed to whatever insights into the meaning of Revelation may be contained in the following pages. Questions from both students and church members, as well as information gleaned from a broad range of commentaries, have helped to bring these chapters to a focus. It is hoped that the first steps undertaken here will kindle in readers a new appreciation for the Book of Revelation, leading to further study of its pages.

The volume is dedicated to my wife, Isobel Mackay Metzger, without whose help and encouragement it would not have been written.

Bruce M. Metzger
Princeton Theological Seminary
Princeton, New Jersey

1

INTRODUCING THE BOOK OF REVELATION

The entire Bible is a library, containing different types of books. Different types of literature make their appeal to the reader through different avenues. For example, the Psalms of David touch one's *emotions*: "Bless the LORD, O my soul, and all that is within me, bless his holy name" (Psalm 103:1). In the Bible are also books of law that involve commands: "Do this!" "Don't do that!" Such books speak to our *will*, requiring us to respond positively or negatively. Still other biblical writings, such as Paul's Letter to the Romans, appeal primarily to our *intellect*. We need to think carefully and patiently as we seek to follow the apostle's theological reasoning.

The Book of Revelation is unique in appealing primarily to our *imagination*—not, however, a freewheeling imagination, but a disciplined imagination. This book contains a series of word pictures, as though a number of slides were being shown upon a great screen. As we watch, we allow ourselves to be carried along by impressions created by these pictures. Many of the details of the pictures are intended to contribute to the total impression and are not to be isolated and interpreted with wooden literalism.

PRELIMINARY CONSIDERATIONS

In order to become oriented to the Book of Revelation one must take seriously what the author says happened. John tells us that he had a series of visions. He says that he "heard" certain words and "saw" certain visions. Over the centuries there have been occasional individuals with the gift of being susceptible to visionary experiences. The author of Revelation seems to have been such a person.

In order to understand what is involved in a visionary experience we may consider Ezekiel's vision of a valley full of dry bones (Ezekiel 37:1-4). In this vision the prophet saw the assembling of the bones into skeletons and the coming of sinews and flesh, climaxed by restoration to life, so that "they lived, and stood on their feet, a vast multitude" (Ezekiel 37:10). We are not to understand that bones were actually scattered around in a valley; the account is purely symbolic. The prophet's visionary experience pictured the revival of the dead nation of Israel, hopelessly scattered in exile. Through this vision, Ezekiel was assured that the dispersed Israelites, living as exiles in foreign lands, would be reestablished as a nation in their own land.

The Acts of the Apostles reports several instances of visionary experiences (9:10; 10:11; 16:9; 18:9; 22:17; compare 27:23). One of the most significant was the apostle Peter's experience at the house of Simon, a tanner, in Joppa. In this case a natural cause cooperated in producing the vision. Hungry, and waiting for a meal to be prepared, Peter fell into a trance and saw "something like a large sheet coming down, being lowered to the ground by its four corners" (Acts 10:11). In it were all kinds of quadrupeds, reptiles, and birds, both fit and unfit for food according to Jewish law and custom. The vision was accompanied by a heavenly voice bidding Peter to slaughter and eat what was provided (Acts 10:13). Peter objected that he had never before eaten unclean foods. A heavenly voice declared: "What God has made clean, you must not call profane" (Acts 10:15). In what followed, Peter understood that the vision was leading him to accept the Gentile centurion Cornelius's invitation to come to his house and stay as a guest, contrary to dominant Jewish custom regarding boundaries between Jews and Gentiles, resulting in Peter baptizing Cornelius's whole household (Acts 10:17-48). We are not to think that there was literally a sheet filled with various creatures, nor that the vision was primarily about eating.

Similarly, when the Book of Revelation reports that John "saw a beast rising out of the sea, having ten horns and seven heads" (13:1), there is no reason to imagine that such a creature actually existed. Nevertheless, the vision had profound significance for John—and still has for the reader today (see pp. 94–97). Such accounts combine cognitive insight with emotional response. They invite the reader or listener to enter into the experience being recounted and to participate in it, triggering mental images of that which is described.

JOHN'S SYMBOLIC LANGUAGE

In reporting his visionary experiences, John frequently uses symbolic language. Sometimes he explains the meaning of the symbols. Other symbols really need no explanation; for example, the number *seven*. Everyone knows that there are seven days in a week; then another week begins. And so seven means completion or perfection. Other symbols in Revelation can be understood in the light of the symbolism used in the Hebrew Scriptures, particularly the books of Ezekiel, Daniel, and Zechariah. It is clear that John had studied the Old Testament very thoroughly. Of the 404 verses that comprise the twenty-two chapters of the Book of Revelation, 278 verses contain one or more allusions to an Old Testament passage. John had so thoroughly pondered the Old Testament that when it came to recording the import of his visions of God and of heaven, he expressed himself by using phrases borrowed from the prophets of Israel. Therefore, in attempting to understand John's symbolism, we must consider not only the book itself but also his use of the Old Testament.

No doubt some of John's symbols seem exceedingly strange to readers today. For example, the Roman Empire is symbolized as a beast like a leopard with feet like a bear's and a mouth like a lion's mouth (13:2)—all very horrible indeed, as those people who were being persecuted by Rome especially knew well. Such strange beasts were more or less commonplace features in apocalyptic literature—and the Book of Revelation is a notable example of that literary genre. More will be said later about such literature, but for the moment it is sufficient to remind ourselves that we, too, make use of animals as symbols of nations and groups: the British lion, the Russian bear, the American eagle, the Democratic donkey, the Republican elephant. A newspaper cartoonist may show a donkey tugging at one end of a rope and an elephant tugging at the other. Young children or new immigrants may not understand that symbolism. Later, they will recognize the competition within a two-party system. In the same way, some of the imagery in Revelation may seem unusual or even bizarre, but on further reflection, and with the use of a disciplined imagination, the meaning will usually become clear. In any case, it is important to recognize that the descriptions are *descriptions of symbols, not of the reality conveyed by the symbols*.

IDENTITY OF THE AUTHOR

The author four times calls himself "John" (1:1, 4, 9; 22:8). This name was common among Jews from the time of the Exile onward and among the early Christians. Four persons are mentioned in the New Testament who bore this name. Which of these is intended, or whether the author was some other early Christian leader with this name, has been extensively debated. The absence of any specific data in the book itself makes it difficult to come to a firm decision. Since there is no qualifying identification (such as "John the elder" or "John Mark"), it is probable that the author feels himself to be well known to his hearers in the seven congregations that he addresses.

From the mid-second century onward the book was widely, though not universally, ascribed to the apostle John, the son of Zebedee. This attribution was accepted in the West beginning with Justin Martyr of Rome (AD 150), Irenaeus of Gaul (180), and Tertullian of North Africa (200). In the East, however, apostolic authorship was sometimes rejected, notably by the so-called Alogi (a group of heretics in Asia Minor, about AD 170), as well as by Dionysius, bishop of Alexandria (after 247). Dionysius argued on the basis of differences of vocabulary and grammatical style between the Fourth Gospel and the Apocalypse and believed the latter to be the work of another person named John, whom he nevertheless affirmed as "holy and inspired."[1]

From this point on, the apostolic origin of Revelation was frequently disputed in the East. Eusebius (AD 325) wavered between regarding the book as "recognized" or as "spurious." But after Athanasius of Alexandria (AD 367) and the Latin church under the influence of Augustine toward the end of the fourth century had accepted Revelation in their lists of the canon, the book was no longer officially contested as part of the New Testament. Even though the precise identity of "John" is still debated today, interpretation of the book does not depend on certainty concerning this matter.

TIME OF WRITING OF REVELATION

The Book of Revelation was composed and sent to seven churches in the Roman province of Asia at some point between AD 69 and 96 in order to persuade them that remaining loyal to Christ and bold in their witness to the one God was ultimately the path to victory. John wanted his congregations to resist both the promises that Rome held out to those who would cooperate with its domination and the pressures and persecutions that Rome and its local supporters would inflict on those who resisted and even critiqued its rule and its practices. It is common to hear Revelation described simply as a book written to encourage persecuted Christians. John does indeed hold in memory many Christians who were martyred by the representatives of Roman power (6:9-11; 17:6; 18:24), but it is noteworthy that he only refers to a single martyrdom among the seven congregations he addresses (2:13). Most of the persecution that he envisions is yet to come—and will come in part as a result of his congregations heeding his own call to uncompromising loyalty and witness to the God of Israel and God's Messiah! John is every bit as concerned that some among his congregations either are oblivious to the ills of Roman imperialism (3:1-6, 14-22) or are actively seeking some path of coexistence to hold on to Christ while mingling with their neighbors in idolatrous settings (2:14-16, 20-25).

While some internal evidence can be understood to point to a date around AD 69, it seems more likely that Revelation addresses a situation later in the first century, probably during the reign of the emperor Domitian (AD 81–96). The prominence of the imperial cult—the worship of "the image of the beast"—in Revelation reflects the increased enthusiasm among the seven cities addressed by Revelation for the imperial cult after the end of the brief but devastating civil wars of AD 68–69. Ephesus, the oldest and probably most important Christian center among the seven cities addressed, especially witnessed a renaissance of the cult of the emperors during this time. While the more balanced emperors were a bit embarrassed by the enthusiasm of provincials to worship them while they were alive, some emperors—and Domitian appears to have been one—relished being addressed as "our lord and god." Ephesus made a bid for and won the "honor" of the right to build a grand temple to the living emperor Domitian, inaugurated in AD 90. This was so important to the city that almost all official inscriptions would thenceforth refer to this honor as part of Ephesus's self-identification. Also by this period, all seven cities addressed by Revelation had some combination of temples, altars, and shrines to various emperors and members of their family. Pressure to participate in the imperial cult would never have been greater.

Augustus had granted the Jewish people immunity from the expectation of participating in emperor worship. At first the Roman authorities regarded the Christians as a sect within Judaism. But toward the close of the first century it was becoming clear that the synagogue did not "own" the Christian movement and, thus, the latter did not fall under the former's aegis. Gentile Christians who refused to participate in emperor worship and the cults of the traditional gods therefore exposed themselves to the charge not only of being unpatriotic, but also of being subversive and enemies of the common good. Consequently, at various times and places they suffered persecution because of their faith. This could take the form of harassment or escalate to economic embargo, physical assault, lynching, or official action.

Also favoring the close of the first century as the time of the composition of Revelation is the fact that, according to 2:8-11, the church in Smyrna had been persevering under trials for a long time, whereas according to Polycarp,[2] the bishop of Smyrna in the first half of the second century, the church there did not yet exist until after the time of Paul (that is, in the 60s). Furthermore, in 3:17 the church in Laodicea is described as rich, though this city had been almost completely destroyed by an earthquake in AD 61 (see p. 55). It would have required some decades for the city and its population to recover economically.

One may conclude, therefore, that the Book of Revelation was written toward the end of Domitian's reign, about AD 90–95. This date is corroborated by the testimony of early church fathers, such as Irenaeus (AD 180), Clement of Alexandria (200), Origen (254), and Eusebius (325).

LITERARY GENRE OF THE BOOK

John called his book an "Apocalypse" (or "revelation"), meaning an unveiling, a disclosure (1:1). While the word refers, on the one hand, to divine revelations given and shared in the context of early Christian worship (1 Corinthians 14:6, 26; 2 Corinthians 12:1, 7), it has also come to name a body of literature that shares some common features and literary strategies and that also claims to be, in some form, divine disclosures. We can find some examples of this kind of literature in the Bible, particularly in the second half of the Book of Daniel, and apocalyptic tendencies can be seen in Isaiah 24–27, Ezekiel 38–39, and Zechariah 9–14, where there are frequent references to the approaching "day of the LORD." The genre blossomed, however, in the period between the testaments. Important examples include 1 Enoch, the Apocalypse of Baruch, the Fourth Book of Ezra, the Ascension of Isaiah, the Apocalypse of Zephaniah, and parts of the Sibylline Oracles.[3]

Writings of this sort typically present the dreams, visions, and conversations of the seer with angelic guides and other super-human figures. They typically paint the broader canvas against which the author and the audience live their daily lives, looking both to the grand timetable from before history to the "Day of the Lord" and after and to the spaces beyond human experience (the heavenly realms, the infernal realms, the presently invisible abodes of the spirits). The "bigger picture" provides an interpretative frame that casts the present situation and its challenges in a way that encourages fidelity to the group's faith and practice. These works typically use colorful and figurative language, for example representing kingdoms and people as animals. They typically present the cosmos in starkly dualistic terms—good and evil, often locked in age-long combat, with the authors urging the hearers to align themselves with the former in the struggle. Apocalypses usually contain predictions about the final outcome of human affairs, focusing on the last age of the world, when good will triumph and evil will be judged. Present troubles are represented as "birth pangs" that will usher in the End. God has set a limit to the era of wickedness and will intervene at the appointed time to execute judgment. In the final battle the powers of evil, together with the evil nations they inhabit, will be utterly destroyed. Then a new order will be established, when the End will be as the Beginning, and Paradise will be restored.

OUTLINE OF THE BOOK

The focus of the Book of Revelation is the Second Coming of the Lord Jesus Christ and the definitive establishment of God's kingdom at the end of time. Corresponding to this, the structure of the book involves a series of parallel yet ever-progressing sections. These bring before the reader, over and over again, the struggle of the church and its victory over the world in the providence of God. Recapitulation—introducing the same event several times from different angles—is an important feature of the book, making a linear outline of its events impossible. We find ourselves repeatedly at the "Day of the Lord" (1:7; 6:12-17; 14:14-20; 19:11–20:15) only to return to more visions illuminating the challenges on this side of that day. A number of series of sevens provide an overall sense of linear progression to the book (the seven oracles to the churches, 2:1–3:22; the seven seals, 6:1–8:1; the seven trumpets, 8:1–11:19; the seven bowls, 15:1–16:21), with John pausing to focus his hearers on visions of special importance to their situation (John's commission and the models of witness, 10:1–11:14; the forces of Satan at work in the church's situation and the consequences of various responses, 12:1–14:13; the unveiling of Rome and its imperialist practices, 17:1–18:24; the alternative city of God, 21:1–22:5).[4]

Here and there in John's account of his visionary experiences he uses the word *then*. There is, however, no reason to assume that the order in which John received his visions must be the order in which the contents of the visions are to be fulfilled. In chapter 12, for example, we will find a vision that takes us back to the time of the birth of Jesus. Such features in the book should make us wary of turning Revelation into a kind of almanac or time chart of the last days based on the sequence of the visions that John experienced. Like any good teacher, he knows that repetition is a helpful learning device, and so he repeats his messages more than once from differing points of view.

2

JOHN'S VISION
OF THE HEAVENLY CHRIST

(Revelation 1:1-20)

THE PROLOGUE
(Revelation 1:1-3)

In the opening sentence of the prologue John discloses to the reader the origin and content of his book: "The revelation of Jesus Christ, which God gave him to show his servants what must soon take place; he made it known by sending his angel to his servant John" (1:1). The source of the revelation is God, who speaks through the Son, who shows to God's people the things that are to be. This revelation is a revelation "of Jesus Christ," which can mean either that the revelation was made by Jesus Christ or that it was made about him or that it belongs to him. In a sense all three are true: the revelation comes from God through Jesus Christ, who communicates it to John by an angel. The revelation is Jesus Christ's and the chain of communication is God . . . Jesus Christ . . . angel . . . John . . . to the churches. The purpose of the revelation is to show "what must soon take place." Here the sense of "must" is not the necessity imposed by fate, but the sure fulfillment of the purpose of God. The word *soon* indicates that John intended his message for his own generation.

The material in the Book of Revelation is so important that a blessing[1] is promised to the one who reads it aloud, and to those who hear and who keep what is written in the prophecy (1:3). The word *aloud* is not in the Greek, but is implied. In New Testament times, reading was usually a group activity, with one person reading to others. Not all people, of course, could read; furthermore, manuscripts of books were expensive, and few Christians could afford them. In the absence of printed books, great emphasis was laid in the early church on the public reading of handwritten copies of communications to congregations (Colossians 4:16; 1 Thessalonians 5:27; compare 1 Timothy 4:13). John calls his book *prophecy*; it has the weight of the words of the prophets of the Old Testament. For this reason, therefore, a divine blessing can be pronounced on those who read and who hear the book, and who "keep what is written in it" (1:3)—that is, who align their practices with the book's call to the exclusive worship of the one God and his Messiah and to witness to God's justice in the midst of the unjust practices of empire.

THE SALUTATION: GREETINGS TO THE CHURCHES
(Revelation 1:4-8)

The practical character of the prophetic word (1:3) is implied by the personal greetings that the writer extends to the recipients of his book. The body of Revelation opens in the manner of a typical letter, identifying its immediate recipients as "the seven churches that are in Asia" (1:4). The salutation thus indicates that the entire book, and not merely the portion containing the seven oracles (chapters 2 and 3), is intended for the churches of Asia. "Asia" here refers not to the great continent of that name, but to the Roman province of Asia, located in the western part of modern Turkey. We do not know on what principle the seven churches were selected. There were certainly more than seven churches in the region by the time this book was written, including congregations in Troas, Colossae, and Hierapolis (Acts 20:5-12; Colossians 1:2; 4:13).[2] John may have had a special relationship with these seven. Their arrangement and relative proximity might suggest that John visited them on a regular basis, exhorting and guiding them prior to his exile to Patmos. Since seven is a number often symbolizing completeness, John might have regarded these seven congregations as, in some sense, representative of the whole church.

John opens his communication with a dual salutation, "Grace and peace." The apostle Paul had used this salutation at the beginning of all his letters, and it soon became a traditional greeting among Christians (compare also 1 Peter 1:2 and 2 Peter 1:2). The salutation invokes the grace and peace that come from God, and reminds us of the favor and acceptance that God has extended to believers. And it is because of God's grace that his people can enjoy peace—peace with God as well as the peace of God, resulting in inner poise and tranquility, even amid the hardest experiences of life.

To this dual salutation John adds three phrases identifying the source of the grace and peace. They come, he says, "from him who is and who was and who is to come, and from the seven spirits who are before his throne, and from Jesus Christ" (1:4-5). Greeks had praised their chief god thus: "Zeus was, Zeus is, Zeus shall be. O mighty Zeus!" (Pausanias 10.12.10). John uses the language of God's self-disclosure in Exodus 3:14 (the "I AM," "the One who is") and extends it in polemical competition with pagan claims. God, not Zeus, is the eternal one. In a major twist, John proclaims not merely a God who "shall be," but a God who "is coming"—in judgment upon those who give God's glory to another (9:20-21; 14:6-7).

Grace and peace, John continues, also come "from the seven spirits who are before his throne." It has been popular to understand this to refer to the Holy Spirit, thus finding a reference to the three Persons of the Godhead in this verse. Appeal is often made to Isaiah 11:2 and the "sevenfold" characteristics of the Spirit for support. It is more likely, however, that John refers to the seven angels of the presence, the chief among God's angelic hosts. Several Jewish texts refer to such an order of angels, some quite specifically: "I am Raphael, one of the seven angels who stand ready and enter before the glory of the Lord" (Tobit 12:15, Apocrypha).[3] John himself will shortly speak (again) of "the seven angels who stand before God" in 8:2 in a manner that assumes that the hearers have prior acquaintance with this group. The only available antecedent within Revelation would be the "seven spirits" of Revelation 1:4; 4:5 who are "before his throne." "Angels" and "spirits" are used interchangeably in other texts (Psalm 104:4 and Hebrews 1:7 explicitly equate the two).

Grace and peace also pour down from Jesus Christ, who is described as "the faithful witness, the firstborn of the dead, and the ruler of the kings of the earth" (1:5). In a day when many were suffering because of their Christian witness, it would encourage them to be reminded that Jesus Christ was "the faithful witness" *par excellence* (see 1 Timothy 6:13); as for those inclined to compromise, the example and power of this Christ would give them pause. The following description, "the firstborn of the dead, and the ruler of the kings of the earth," is an echo of Psalm 89:27, where God appoints David (and, by implication, the son of David) "the firstborn, the highest of the kings of the earth." Here John's use of the title "the firstborn" is related to Christ's status in resurrection, as in Colossians 1:18 (compare 1 Corinthians 15:20; also Romans 8:29), anticipating the resurrection of the many sons and daughters.

John's further description of Jesus Christ identifies him as the one "who loves us and freed us from our sins by his blood" (1:5). John reminds his congregations of Jesus' astounding generosity toward and investment in them, allowing his own lifeblood to be poured out to reconcile them to God and break sin's power over them—an act of great love that signals Jesus' ongoing love for them. Such a reminder could not have failed to arouse feelings of gratitude and (re)awakened an obligation of loyalty toward so great a benefactor. Some of the later Greek manuscripts read, "who loves us and washed us from our sins," where the scribes confused the word *lusanti* ("freed") with the word *lousanti* ("washed"). Both readings are theologically significant: believers have been freed from the chain of sin as well as cleansed from the stain of sin.

Christ liberated us to make us "a kingdom, priests serving his God and Father" (1:6). This is the truth that Protestant Reformers emphasized in the doctrine of the universal priesthood of all believers. Through Jesus Christ every Christian has access to God and can intercede on behalf of others. The political implications of this verse, however, should not go unnoticed: John claims the believers' primary political allegiance for God and God's kingdom, a radical claim indeed when Roman power in the Mediterranean and Levant was nearing its peak.

John draws the hearers' attention to the event that they must bear in mind in all of their decision-making in their day-to-day lives: "Look! He is coming with the clouds" (1:7). Christ's return—and its implications for those who have participated in rejecting him and his call—is the primary crisis that they must prioritize and for which they must remain ever prepared. If they keep this day fixed in their mind's eye, what they must do every day will become crystal clear, however costly it might be.

The solemn opening of the book climaxes with God's self-disclosure: "I am the Alpha and the Omega" (1:8). These are the first and last letters of the Greek alphabet, implying that God was before all things and will outlast all things, an idea expressed earlier by Isaiah (44:6). God's eternity and forthcoming intervention in human affairs are brought out once again by the addition of the statement, "who is and who was and who is to come, the Almighty" (Revelation 1:8).

JOHN'S FIRST VISION: THE GLORIFIED CHRIST
(Revelation 1:9-20)

John introduces his first vision by telling his readers that he was on the island of Patmos because he had proclaimed God's message and the truth that Jesus revealed (1:9-10). Patmos is a rocky, mountainous island, about ten miles long and six miles wide, some thirty miles west of Asia Minor in the Aegean Sea.

The Romans used such islands as places of political banishment. Patmos was far from barren, however. It was home to temples to Artemis and Apollo and a community large enough to support a gymnasium (an educational as well as athletic facility). It had several ports that could be used by mariners and merchants traveling across the Aegean.

How long John had been on Patmos we do not know, but he tells us that on a certain Lord's day he fell into a trance and was caught up in the spirit. A trumpet-like voice behind him said, "Write[4] in a book what you see and send it to the seven churches, to Ephesus, to Smyrna, to Pergamum, to Thyatira, to Sardis, to Philadelphia, and to Laodicea" (1:11).

Why do the names of the churches stand in their present order? Some have suggested that the messages sent to them depict successively the status and conditions of the church at important stages down through the ages. But there is not the slightest indication in the text that this is so.[5] The reason for the present order is much more simple: it is the order in which, starting from Ephesus (the city closest to Patmos), a messenger carrying the book would travel, somewhat in a semicircle, going successively to each of the churches. The average distance between each locality is between twenty-five and fifty miles. A glance at a map (see p. 26) will show that the seven cities are so situated as to be centers from which the book could be circulated through a very wide expanse of country.

Having heard the trumpet-like voice behind him, John turned and beheld the heavenly Christ in majestic, breathtaking splendor. This is how he describes his vision:

> *I saw seven golden lampstands,[6] and in the midst of the lampstands I saw one like the Son of Man, clothed with a long robe and with a golden sash across his chest. His head and his hair were white as white wool, white as snow; his*

eyes were like a flame of fire, his feet were like burnished bronze, refined as in a furnace, and his voice was like the sound of many waters. In his right hand he held seven stars, and from his mouth came a sharp, two-edged sword, and his face was like the sun shining with full force.

(1:12-16)

How shall we understand this description of the heavenly Christ? It may seem paradoxical to say that the description does not mean what it says; it means what it means. We note first that the writer explains part of the symbolism at the end of the chapter: "the seven lampstands are the seven churches" (1:20). Therefore when John says he saw Christ in the midst of the lampstands, he wants to let us know that Christ is not an absentee landlord. On the contrary, he is in the midst of his churches, supporting them during trials and persecutions, goading them in the midst of their temptations to compromise their witness and practice. Furthermore, when John describes Christ as wearing a long robe with a golden sash across his chest, he presents Christ in kingly array.

When we read that Christ has hair like white wool, white as snow, John does not mean that the Lord is prematurely aged. This description is taken from a passage in Daniel (7:9) where the prophet describes his vision of God, the Ancient of Days. In this way John assigns a dignity to Christ in terms that resemble Daniel's vision of God Almighty. Piercing eyes "like a flame of fire" burn away our shams and hypocrisies, looking into our innermost selves. Feet "like burnished bronze" represent strength and stability (contrast Daniel 2:33, 41). John describes the voice of Christ as penetrating and unmistakable, "like the sound of many waters," words that the prophet Ezekiel used to describe the God of Israel (Ezekiel 43:2 RSV). The meaning of the seven stars that Christ holds in his right hand is explained at the end of the chapter; they "are the angels of the seven churches" (1:20). The sword that comes from his mouth symbolizes his word of judgment (see Hebrews 4:12). Finally, John says that the face of Christ is like the sun shining with full strength. This, John says, is the Lord whom we serve! This is the genuine Son of God whose glory and power make a mockery of the pretensions of the emperors who called themselves "son of the divine Augustus" and the like!

Instead of taking John's account with flat-footed literalism, we should imaginatively allow ourselves to be guided by the poetic quality of the narrative. We trivialize the account if we make a composite picture of the heavenly Christ showing each of these features literalistically. One should think of it like this: a young man writes a love letter to his fiancée, describing how charming she is. Her eyes, he says, are like limpid pools of water, her cheeks are like rose petals, and her neck is graceful, like the neck of a swan. If someone were to draw a picture, literalistically depicting all these features, the young woman certainly would not feel flattered! So too, John's description of the heavenly Christ does not mean what it says; it means what it means.

In the presence of such a sublime and wonderful experience, John is overcome with awe, and he falls down "as though dead" (1:17). But he is quickly made to stand up again by the touch of Christ's right hand—for the whole point of the vision is not to overwhelm John, but to reassure him by showing Christ resplendent with divine attributes. After bidding John not to be afraid, Christ identifies himself, saying, "I am the first and the last, and the living one. I was dead, and see, I am alive forever and ever; and I have the keys of Death and of Hades" (1:17-18). In these three statements the seer is assured that the heavenly Christ bears the same titles as does the Lord God, the Almighty (see v. 8), and that after Jesus had conquered death, he is preeminently "the living one . . . alive forever and ever." To "have the keys of Death and of Hades" is to possess authority over their domain. Death and Hades together express one idea, the realm of the departed. Christ's holding the "keys" gives John's hearers the assurance they need when threatened with death because of their loyalty to him. They need not fear: Christ has the authority and power to unlock the gate of death for his faithful ones.

At the conclusion of the vision, John receives the command to write "what you have seen, what is, and what is to take place after this" (1:19). What John has seen embraced both the situation already in existence and things that still lie in the future. One of the chief problems in the interpretation of the Book of Revelation is to distinguish between those elements in John's visions that symbolize "what is" from those that symbolize "what is to take place after this" (1:19).

3

PROPHETIC WORDS TO THE CHURCHES

(Revelation 2:1-29)

In chapter 1, the heavenly Christ revealed himself to John and commissioned him to bear his prophetic words to his congregations. These two chapters present the messages that Christ directs to each of seven churches in the Roman province of Asia, located in the western part of Asia Minor. By the 90s of the first century there were many more than seven churches in western Asia Minor. Besides those mentioned here, we know from Paul's letters the names of several other cities in which there were Christian congregations. Why, we may ask, were no messages written to them? It may be, of course, that John was acquainted with just these seven.

On the other hand, since seven is a very special number, meaning complete, all-inclusive, it appears that, by identifying just seven churches, John wishes to suggest that the messages are relevant to all churches, wherever they may be located.

These are often referred to as "letters" to the seven churches, but this does not accurately reflect their form or their nature. Each begins with a command to John to write down the words that he hears spoken, but the words themselves begin in a manner reminiscent of the prophetic oracles of the Hebrew prophets. "Thus says the Lord" has become "these are the words of him who holds the seven stars," or some other descriptive identification of the glorified Christ who utters these pronouncements.

The seven oracles follow a shared pattern. Each message begins with the heavenly Christ identifying himself, typically using one or another of the various features from the symbolic description of Christ in chapter 1. Thus, the first letter is introduced by the statement, "These are the words of him who holds the seven stars in his right hand, who walks among the seven golden lampstands" (2:1, compare 1:20), a declaration of Christ's continuing presence with and oversight of his people. The message continues, if applicable, with a statement concerning what the congregation is doing or has done well, such that its Lord can commend it, followed by a diagnosis of how the congregation or some part thereof has fallen short of Christ's expectations. Each concludes, then, with warnings concerning the consequences of not amending what is amiss, promises to those who successfully "overcome" or "conquer" the challenges to faithfulness in their setting, and a charge to "listen to what the Spirit is saying to the churches" (2:7, 11, 17, 29; 3:6; 13; 22). The word *conquer* is a military term. It suggests that the Christian life, so far from being a bed of roses, involves a struggle against anyone and anything that saps the Christian life and witness of all that gives it its distinctive character and power.

The message of each of the seven letters is directed to the "angel" of the particular church. The term *angel* could denote the local church leader, or it could refer to the spiritual guardian angel of that church. Certainly the consistent usage of the word elsewhere in the book argues strongly for the latter view. The idea that each congregation had its angelic overseer is consistent with the belief in guardian angels for individuals (see Matthew 18:10; Acts 12:14-15) and angelic overseers for nations (Daniel 12:1). It is clear, however, that the words are meant for the Christians themselves, as the forms of address frequently slip from the singular address to an angel to a plural address to the whole audience (as in Revelation 2:10).

THE ORACLE TO THE CHURCH IN EPHESUS
(Revelation 2:1-7)

Ephesus was the principal city of Asia Minor, with a population of about 250,000. It was wealthy and cosmopolitan. Trade passed through it by land and water, as it was the major commercial hub and seaport for the region. Ephesus had become an epicenter of imperial cult in Asia Minor, with a local temple to "the Goddess *Roma* and the Divine Augustus" and a provincial temple to the emperor Domitian. It was also home to one of the seven wonders of the ancient world: the temple of Diana (or Artemis, as she was called by the Greeks), the great mother goddess. Ancient descriptions of the temple testify to the architectural grandeur of the building. Its roof was held over sixty feet aloft, resting upon over a hundred columns and covering a space greater than twice the size of an American football field. The internal ornamentation was of extraordinary splendor, adorned by works of art created by famous Greek artists. From all parts of the Mediterranean world, tourists and devotees came to view and to worship in the great temple.

The Christian faith was established at Ephesus in the 50s of the first century. Paul had spent three years there during his third missionary journey (Acts 20:31). One result of his preaching was the reduction in the sale of silver souvenirs of the temple of Diana. The Book of Acts (19:21-41) tells of the uproar that occurred when the guild of silversmiths, fearful that their sales would keep falling away, started a riot in order to prevent further Christian influence from hurting their business.

On a subsequent visit, Paul warned the elders of the church at Ephesus that they would face times of trial: "I know that after I have gone, savage wolves will come in among you, not sparing the flock. Some even from your own group will come distorting the truth in order to entice the disciples to follow them" (Acts 20:29-30). Paul's warnings had proven true, but the oracle in Revelation 2 describes how the Christians in Ephesus had resisted the false teachers that had arisen: "I know your works, your toil and your patient endurance. I know that you cannot tolerate evildoers; you have tested those who claim to be apostles but are not, and have found them to be false" (2:2).

These words of praise are followed by words of rebuke: "But I have this against you, that you have abandoned the love you had at first" (2:4). The Ephesians had made a good start. They had weeded out those who were spreading ideas that did not ring true according to the apostolic faith.[1] But the weeding-out process had been achieved at a high cost. The love they had at first had grown cold. It is unclear whether love for Christ, love for one another, or love for the outsider is meant (possibly all three). It is clear, however, that careful orthodoxy without generous love (like the reverse) leaves a church vulnerable before Christ's scrutiny.

Therefore the heavenly Christ warns the readers: "Repent, and do the works you did at first. If not, I will come to you and remove your lampstand from its place, unless you repent" (2:5). The very future of the congregation and its witness (its "light") is at stake: the zeal to find the right way and a commitment to the way of loving must be held together.

The letter concludes with an exhortation and a promise: "Let anyone who has an ear listen to what the Spirit is saying to the churches" (2:7). Of course everyone has ears, but the sense here is that everyone who has spiritual perception should listen. This summons to hear and to *heed* the instructions of the oracle recalls Jesus' own idiom when teaching (see Mark 4:9, 23), helping the Christians to recognize the voice of their Shepherd addressing them from beyond this realm. The promise is, "To everyone who conquers, I will give permission to eat from the tree of life that is in the paradise of God" (Revelation 2:7). The tree of life, which had been denied to Adam (Genesis 3:22), is now accessible to the conqueror; to the person, that is, who obeys the message of the letter and overcomes the challenges to faithful witness and obedience in his or her setting.

THE ORACLE TO THE CHURCH IN SMYRNA
(Revelation 2:8-11)

The messenger, traveling about thirty-five miles north from Ephesus, would reach another of the great cities of Asia Minor—Smyrna (modern Izmir). A city of great antiquity, Smyrna became a large and prosperous commercial center. The city was renowned for its loyalty to Rome and its ritual worship of the emperor. In 195 BC, almost three hundred years before the writing of

Revelation, the people of Smyrna dedicated the world's first temple to the goddess Roma. In AD 26, almost seventy years before John's banishment, Smyrna dedicated a magnificent temple in honor of the emperor Tiberius, winning it the title of *neokoros*, or "temple warden," of a provincial imperial cult. The letter to the church in Smyrna is the shortest of the seven messages and, like the letter to the church in Philadelphia, contains no rebuke, only commendation. The Christians at Smyrna had to endure persecution and deprivation, due no doubt to their refusal to take part in ceremonies connected with emperor worship. Their fidelity to the worship of the one God and to Jesus brought them to economic hardship; the local Jewish community appears to have increased their vulnerability by making it clear to the local authorities that the Christians (with their revolutionary gospel!) were not a part of the Jewish community. This seems to be the likeliest explanation for "the slander on the part of those who say that they are Jews" (2:9). The label "synagogue of Satan" (also v. 9) strikes modern ears as especially harsh in a post-Holocaust world, but it was not unprecedented in inner-Jewish debate. The community at Qumran associated with the Dead Sea Scrolls, for example, considered other Jews outside their sect to be "a congregation of Beliar," another name for Satan.[2]

Christ exhorts these persecuted believers to be faithful to the extent of being ready to die for his sake (2:10). Opposition to the gospel would become so fierce that martyrdom appeared to be a real possibility. Indeed, one of the best-known Christian martyrs of all ages was a native of Smyrna—Polycarp, bishop of Smyrna, executed in AD 156 (see the account in the *Martyrdom of Polycarp*).

To the faithful at Smyrna who do not flinch, Christ promises to give "the crown of life" (2:10). In Greek there are two words that can be translated "crown." One is *diadema*, which means a royal crown; the other, which is used here, is *stephanos*, which usually has something to do with joy and victory. John is referring to the wreaths that were presented to the winners at the Olympic and other games.

To the faithful another promise is made: they "will not be harmed by the second death" (2:11). What is the second death? Our first death happens when we take our last breath on earth. The second death comes to impenitent sinners at the Final Judgment. Later in this book (see p. 125), John is more specific about what this involves, and who will suffer it (20:6, 14; 21:8; compare also the words of Jesus in Matthew 10:28 and Luke 12:4-5).

THE ORACLE TO THE CHURCH IN PERGAMUM
(Revelation 2:12-17)

Pergamum, about fifty miles north of Smyrna, was a city that had many claims to distinction. Since the second century before Christ, it was the capital of the Roman province of Asia. No traveler could visit Pergamum without being impressed by its welter of temples and altars. The greater part of the city stood in the shadow of a great hill that was dotted with dozens of temples to pagan gods. Prominently set on a terrace near the top of the hill stood an immense altar to Zeus. The altar stood on a huge platform surrounded by colonnades, and the whole structure looked like an enormous throne. On this platform, animal sacrifices were burned twenty-four hours a day by a constantly changing team of priests. The overpowering smell of burning animal flesh permeated the air in Pergamum, and all day long a column of smoke could be seen from miles around, serving to keep the supremacy of Zeus ever in the public eye. This remains the likeliest landmark that the

Glorified Christ had in mind when he spoke of "Satan's throne" (2:13). This is all the more likely as Jews commonly identified the pagan gods with demons—who better to identify Zeus, the chief of the gods, with than Satan, the chief of the demons?

Pergamum was also a center for the worship of the emperors. The city was awarded the honor of building a temple to Augustus and the goddess *Roma* in 29 BC, making it the first among the seven cities addressed by Revelation to become the *neokoros* (the "temple warden") of an imperial cult. The city was also renowned for its extensive Asclepion, a shrine to Asclepius, the god of healing. Sanatoria were attached to the temples where the sick were laid in the hope that one of the sacred snakes would touch and heal them. The serpent was Asclepius's symbol, and it is still depicted in the caduceus, the insignia of medical associations. To John, however, the serpent was a symbol of the personification of evil, "that ancient serpent, who is called the Devil and Satan" (12:9). Temples of Athena, Dionysus, Hera, and Demeter have also been identified on the acropolis. It is possible, then, that John was referring to the city as "Satan's throne" in a more general way, in view of such a multiplicity of forms of paganism.

Pergamum was not an easy city for Christians to live in, and it must have been a great comfort for believers there to know that the Lord knew what they were experiencing. Hostility to the church was determined and more vicious in Pergamum than in many other towns. There had been real persecution, and a believer named Antipas had been killed—whether formally or as a result of a lynch mob—in order to persuade the others to forsake their faith, and to discourage others from becoming Christians (2:13).

The church, however, needed help not only against enemies outside but also against enemies within. Some members held "to the teaching of the Nicolaitans" (2:15). The sect whose works the

44

church at Ephesus had resisted (2:6) had also made inroads at Pergamum. The glorified Christ describes them as teaching his servants to "eat food sacrificed to idols and practice fornication" (2:14). Eating meat was a tricky business in the ancient world. A great deal of the meat for sale in the market places came from the flesh of sacrificial animals. A token portion of the animal was offered to the god and the larger part made available for purchase (a significant source of revenue for the temples). The Jerusalem church had earlier required Gentile converts to abstain from food sacrificed to idols (Acts 15:29). However, Christians interpreted this advice in different ways. Paul clearly regarded it as meaning that believers should not take part in sacrificial meals held at pagan shrines, but were otherwise free to eat whatever was put in front of them and to buy whatever was sold in the market (1 Corinthians 8:7-13; 10:20-21). The Nicolaitans appear to have justified Christian participation in idolatrous rituals and settings, which would have greatly eased their negotiating life in the midst of their cities and neighbors. John condemned this, however, as spiritual fornication, a gross act of infidelity toward the God who created and Christ who redeemed them. The Lord tells them to repent; otherwise they will be punished (2:16).

To those who stand firm against both persecution and false teachings the Lord promises to give some of the hidden manna (2:17). Manna was the food supplied by God to the Israelites during their long journey from Egypt to the Promised Land (Exodus 16:32-34). Besides the hidden manna, the heavenly Christ promises to "give a white stone, and on the white stone is written a new name that no one knows except the one who receives it" (2:17). In ancient times a white stone was greatly prized, either as an amulet, especially if the name of some deity was engraved upon it, or as a mark of membership in a special group.

THE ORACLE TO THE CHURCH IN THYATIRA
(Revelation 2:18-29)

Thyatira, about forty-five miles southeast on the road from Pergamum to Sardis, was a town of considerable commercial importance in which there were many traders and artisans. Ancient records indicate the presence there of many trade guilds. Archaeologists have found inscriptions that mention guilds of wool workers, linen workers, makers of outer garments, dyers, leather-workers, tanners, potters, bakers, slave dealers, and bronzesmiths. Such guilds combined some of the features of our modern trade unions with certain religious features. Banquets of the members of the guild often took place within a pagan temple or shrine, where an animal was offered to the gods and then eaten by the members of the guild.

This obviously put Christians in a difficult dilemma. If they did not participate in such feasts and ceremonies of the guild, they would find it more challenging to make a living, as the business and social networks offered by the guild brought significant advantage. If they did participate, however, they were being unfaithful to the Lord who called for exclusive worship and the witness this bore.

Christ begins the letter to Thyatira by commending the devout Christians there for their efforts to remain faithful: "I know your works—your love, faith, service, and patient endurance" (2:19). It is good to read, "I know that your last works are greater than the first." There is progress in the life of this congregation, which forms a contrast to the church in Ephesus where the members are reprimanded for having fallen back (2:4). There is much to commend at Thyatira.

At the same time, the church at Thyatira was guilty of tolerating a woman "who calls herself a prophet" (2:20). John identifies her with the name of her Old Testament counterpart, Jezebel, Ahab's Phoenician queen, who corrupted the faith of Israel with "the many whoredoms and sorceries" of her native gods, Baal and Astarte (2 Kings 9:22; compare 1 Kings 16:31-33). The heavenly Christ had called the would-be prophet to repentance, but she refused "to repent of her fornication" (Revelation 2:21). The word *fornication* is probably used here, as in the oracle to Pergamum, in the Old Testament sense of apostasy and spiritual infidelity. Her teaching of what the writer witheringly calls "the deep things of Satan" (2:24) had the effect of compromising Christian commitment by taking part in pagan practices. We should not minimize the importance of problems confronting first-century Christians, for it was economic suicide to reject the minimum requirements for guild membership. Nor should we dismiss this problem as only of academic interest, as if it does not concern us. Every generation of Christians must face the question: How far should I accept and adopt contemporary standards and practices in business, social arrangements, and the like?

To the usual phrase, "everyone who conquers," there is added "and continues to do my works to the end" (2:26) where "my works" is contrasted with "her doings." "To the end" suggests that perseverance in the Christian life is all-important.

Two rewards are promised to those who conquer: they will share in Christ's messianic rule over the nations (2:26), and to them Christ will give the morning star (2:28). The promise of the gift of the morning star is, of course, not to be understood literalistically as the bestowal of millions of tons of celestial matter; the expression is a metaphor announcing the dawn of a new day and the fulfillment of hope after the night of longing and expectation. In fact, John's symbolism of "morning star" is indicated at the very end of his book where the Lord describes himself as "the bright morning star" (22:16). In pledging to give this star to the conqueror, Christ is pledging to give himself. The ultimate reward enjoyed by Christians is to be with their Lord.

4

MORE PROPHETIC WORDS TO CHURCHES

(Revelation 3:1-22)

THE ORACLE TO THE CHURCH IN SARDIS
(Revelation 3:1-6)

Sardis, a busy commercial and industrial city at the junction of five roads about thirty miles south of Thyatira, had been the capital of the ancient region called Lydia. In the sixth century BC, it was one of the greatest cities of the world, where the fabulous King Croesus reigned amid his treasures. Even though the citadel of Sardis was situated on an almost impregnable hill with sheer cliffs on three sides that dropped some fifteen hundred feet to the valley below, the city had twice suffered humiliating defeats. In the sixth century BC, because of lack of vigilance, the city experienced a stealthy attack by the Persians, and once again, through the negligence of its defenders, Sardis was captured by Antiochus the Great in 214 BC. Still later in its history, in AD 17 the city was devastated by a catastrophic earthquake. Through the generosity of the emperor Tiberius, who remitted the taxes for five years, the city was rebuilt and began once again to flourish as a woolen center. Although the city had lost most of its former glory, it was still known for its wealth and its luxurious and licentious living.

To the church in Sardis, Christ presents himself as the one who has "the seven spirits of God and the seven stars" (3:1). These words indicate his sovereign control over churches and the source of spiritual power. The church at Sardis needed just such a reminder, for this congregation, though having a "name of being alive," was in fact "dead" (3:1). No rebuke could be sharper; the church was an example of merely nominal Christianity.

And yet the Lord does not begin the letter with threats; he begins with a series of urgent admonitions: "Wake up, and strengthen what remains. . . . Remember then what you received and heard; obey it, and repent" (3:2-3). Here are five staccato imperatives: Wake up! Strengthen what remains! Remember! Obey! Repent!

As the city had fallen in the past because of lack of vigilance, so now the Sardians are reminded to be watchful and to shake off their apathy. If, however, they "do not wake up," Christ says, "I will come like a thief," that is to say, he will come when he is not being expected. The language is strongly reminiscent of Jesus' own words concerning his coming again and the need for watchfulness so as to be prepared (see Matthew 24:43-44; compare 1 Thessalonians 5:2-5; Revelation 16:15).

The situation at Sardis was critical but not hopeless. There were "still a few persons in Sardis who had not soiled their clothes" (3:4). Archaeologists have found inscriptions posted in pagan shrines in Asia Minor that indicate that those who wore dirty clothing were excluded from worship because they were an insult to the gods. But the meaning here is probably symbolic, with clothes symbolizing the purity of their Christian life (see Zechariah 3:3-5). Rubbing shoulders too closely with the paganism and the economic injustices of the Roman administration of Sardis would contaminate again the lives that Jesus had died to cleanse.

Christ's promise to the faithful few is that henceforth "they will walk with me, dressed in white, for they are worthy" (3:4). Members of the Jewish sect of the Essenes at Qumran wore white garments as a symbol of their inner purity. White was the color used by the Roman emperor in a triumphal procession. In the Old Testament white garments signify heaven (Daniel 7:9) and festivity (Ecclesiastes 9:8). All these symbols are included here with the emphasis on victory: "If you conquer, you will be clothed like them in white robes" (3:5).

A further promise made by Christ to faithful Christians is phrased negatively: "I will not blot your name out of the book of life" (3:5). In ancient cities the names of citizens were kept in registers and were erased upon death or the commission of a treasonous act. The idea of writing names in the book of life had a long history in Judaism. Moses prayed that if God would not forgive the sin of the Israelites in the golden calf episode, he wished to be blotted out "of the book that you have written" (Exodus 32:32; compare Psalm 69:28). By the time of Daniel, the theme had developed to include the idea of books being opened on the day of judgment (Daniel 7:10; 12:1). The idea of a divine register is found frequently in the New Testament; it is referred to by Jesus (Luke

10:20), Paul (Philippians 4:3), and especially John, who often refers to such records (Revelation 3:5; 13:8; 17:8; 20:12,15; 21:27), but says nothing about the manner in which they are kept.

The final promise is directed to those who conquer, "I will confess your name before my Father and before his angels" (3:5), and is a repetition of Jesus' pronouncement in the Gospels that he would acknowledge those who acknowledge him before others (Matthew 10:32; Luke 12:8). The concluding words of the letter are thus a challenge to the readers to be faithful.

THE ORACLE TO THE CHURCH IN PHILADELPHIA
(Revelation 3:7-13)

Philadelphia was about thirty-five miles southeast of Sardis. The city had been founded in the second century BC by Attalus II Philadelphos, one of the kings of Pergamum, and was the youngest of the seven cities. *Philadelphos* is the Greek word that means "one who loves his brother." Such was the affection of Attalus for his brother Eumenes that he was called Philadelphos, and it was after him that Philadelphia was named.

The ancient historian Strabo called Philadelphia "a city full of earthquakes." Earth tremors were frequent and had caused many former inhabitants to leave the city for a safer home in the surrounding country. The severe earthquake of AD 17, which had devastated Sardis, almost completely demolished Philadelphia. But by the 90s, with the aid of an imperial subsidy, Philadelphia had been rebuilt, and within the city there was a congregation of Christian believers.

The church in Philadelphia was very different from the church in Sardis. It was poor, small, and harassed both by pagan citizens and by the local synagogue, but its members had not strayed from the way. The letter to Sardis contains almost unmitigated censure; the letter to Philadelphia is one of unqualified commendation. The opening formula, "I know your works," is followed by no word of reproof but by the declaration, "I have set before you an open door" (3:8). What is this door that has been opened wide and that "no one is able to shut"? In Christian understanding, a "door" was a technical expression for an opportunity for spreading the gospel (see 1 Corinthians 16:9; 2 Corinthians 2:12; Colossians 4:3). The church, though small, had a great missionary task to perform.

The missionary zeal of the church, however, had been met with opposition. The source of this opposition appeared to have come from the Jewish population of the city, who rejected the claim of Christians to be the spiritual Israel. Since John himself had been born a Jew, we must not take the expression "those of the synagogue of Satan" (3:9) in an anti-Jewish or anti-Semitic sense. The synagogue at Philadelphia was criticized, not for being Jewish, but for being hostile to Christians. The authorities of the synagogue may by this time have formally excommunicated any of their group who confessed Jesus as the Messiah. The so-called "Benediction against heretics" was already being promulgated throughout the synagogues as the Jewish people sought to define themselves—and their boundaries—more clearly. Never mind, says Christ; the time will come when those who have resisted the gospel will yet recognize the church as the true "Israel of God" (see Galatians 6:16) and "will learn that I have loved you" (3:9).

A reward is promised to this little church. Because it had faithfully kept "my word of patient endurance," Christ says, "I will keep you from the hour of trial that is coming on the whole world to test the inhabitants of the earth" (3:10). The phrase "the inhabitants of the earth" is an expression used elsewhere in Revelation to refer to the enemies of the church. This is the first indication in the book of an approaching general visitation, which will be portrayed in the successive series of judgment-visions from Revelation chapter 6 onward. It is not easy to determine whether the promise, "I will keep you from the hour of trial" (3:10), means "keep you from undergoing the trial" or "keep you throughout the trial." But the promise can scarcely mean entire escape from suffering, because the promise to the one who conquers (v. 12) shows that there will be martyrs. It appears, therefore, that the Philadelphia church will not be spared from testing. It will be kept *in and through,* not *from,* the time of trouble.

The special reward promised to the one who conquers is addressed (as in each of the seven letters) to the individual members of the church: "I will make you a pillar in the temple of my God; you will never go out of it" (3:12). The idea of making the victor a pillar in God's temple is clearly symbolic, for later in the book John will insist that there is no need for a temple in God's city (21:22). John is not concerned to keep the details of one vision consistent with those of another. In each he is making a point with emphasis, and we should not try to dovetail one vision into the details of another. Apocalyptic imagery is sufficiently fluid to allow the figure of a temple in one vision and to dismiss it in another.

The metaphor of a pillar in God's temple can be understood either as a pillar supporting the roof of the sanctuary, or as a freestanding pillar as a lasting monument. It was customary to erect such pillars or columns with inscriptions to celebrate the lives or victories of great leaders. In any case, the point seems to be that the pillar will not be moved from its base, as had happened to many pillars in earthquake prone Philadelphia.

The letter closes with the same exhortation that appears at the end of each letter, "Let anyone who has an ear listen to what the

Spirit is saying to the churches" (3:13). The message to each church is at the same time a message to all churches and heard by all the churches, who will therefore witness to one another's honor if they heed, or shame if they ignore, these prophetic oracles.

THE ORACLE TO THE CHURCH IN LAODICEA
(Revelation 3:14-22)

Laodicea completed the semicircle of cities to which, starting at Ephesus, a person would have traveled in order to deliver the seven messages. It was about one hundred miles east of Ephesus and about forty miles southeast of Philadelphia. The city was founded about the middle of the third century BC by Antiochus II of Syria and named in honor of his wife Laodice.

Laodicea was one of the richest commercial centers of Asia Minor. A severe earthquake devastated the city in AD 61, but so rich and independent were its citizens that they refused financial assistance from the Roman government, and out of their own resources and by their own efforts they eventually rebuilt their city. Laodicea was noted for its textile products; the local wool, said to be even softer than that of Miletus, was raven-black in color. The city was also the chief medical center of Phrygia and was famous for its eye salve, which was exported far and wide.

Laodicea, Hierapolis, and Colossae formed a cluster of cities that were evangelized in the 50s during Paul's Ephesian ministry (Acts 19:10)—not by Paul in person but, as it appears, by his colleague, Epaphras (Colossians 4:12-13). Paul, however, regarded those cities as part of his appointed mission field (Colossians 2:1), and asked the Colossian Christians to convey his greetings to believers in Laodicea—among whom "Nympha and the church in her house" are specially mentioned (Colossians 4:15).

By the 90s of the first century the spiritual condition of the church in Laodicea had deteriorated sadly. The decline of the church may have been due in part to the material wealth of its members and to the luxury of their lifestyle. In any case, this church receives the severest condemnation of the seven to which John is bidden to write.

As in the other letters, the heavenly Christ is introduced by a brief description that accents his mysterious divine-human personality. To the Laodiceans he writes as "the Amen" (3:14). This Hebrew word is familiar to us through its use at the end of prayers. But its meaning here, somewhat different from the liturgical use, is brought out by the words that immediately follow, "the faithful and true witness" (3:14). The title may have been suggested by Isaiah 65:16, where "God of faithfulness" would be literally translated "God of Amen." Jesus Christ is the perfect Amen of God, whose words and promises are true beyond all doubt. Christ is further identified as "the origin of God's creation" (3:14). He is not part of the creation, but is the moving cause behind all creation (see John 1:3; 1 Corinthians 8:6; Colossians 1:15, 18).

The solemnity of such titles enhances the sternness of Christ's reproof of the Laodicean church. The reprimand is the most severe in the seven oracles, with no word of commendation. The church is accused of being neither hot nor cold, but of being lukewarm (3:15-16). It is commonly said that John is using local language here, contrasting the tepid water that flowed from Laodicea's aqueducts with the therapeutic hot springs of neighboring Hierapolis and refreshing cold streams of nearby Colossae. Another background for these images might be found in common banqueting practices, in which cold and hot drinks were served as treats in the course of the evening, while tepid water was provided as an emetic to make room for the next course! Either background brings the point home: tepid religion is nauseating. The Lord of the church expresses in the strongest way his repudiation of the church by the warning, "I am about to spit you out of my mouth" (3:16). Their boast of material sufficiency ("You say, 'I am rich, I have prospered, and I need nothing'") is deceptive, and shows a proud, smug self-complacency. Materially affluent and self-satisfied, the church is spiritually "wretched, pitiable, poor, blind, and naked" (3:17). There is some irony in these words, which contrast sharply with the achievements at Laodicea in banking, medicine, and the manufacture of clothing.

To such a church Christ gives his solemn admonition, "I counsel you to buy from me gold refined by fire" (3:18). The parallel with Isaiah 55:1, "You that have no money,...Come, buy wine and milk without money and without price," shows that "buying" is figurative for obtaining. Christ admonishes the church to realize that it is actually poor in spirituality and that it needs to obtain from him the gifts that cannot be purchased with money.

Somewhat abruptly, the speaker changes from harsh denunciation to expressions of affection and tender concern. The proper response to divine correction is to "be earnest, therefore, and repent" (Revelation 3:19). This is the fifth call to repentance in these letters (see 2:5, 16, 21; 3:3); Smyrna and Philadelphia alone needed no such admonition. Laodicea's repentance would involve the replacement of complacency with zealous concern.

To the call to repentance Christ adds the most intimate promise found in any of the seven oracles. "Listen! I am standing at the door, knocking; if you hear my voice and open the door, I will come in to you and eat with you, and you with me" (3:20). Christ's knocking on the door is a simple but profound picture of grace and free will in action. The scene has been unforgettably captured by Holman Hunt in his famous painting, *The Light of the World*.

The Lord has come and is knocking at the door, but there is no handle or latch on the outside of the door; it must be opened from within. The image of eating with the Lord symbolizes the joy of fellowship. In the ancient Near East the sharing of a common meal indicates the forming of a strong bond of affection and companionship. As such it became a common symbol of the intimacy to be enjoyed in the coming messianic kingdom.

The concluding promise belongs to the coming age and is limited to those who conquer, that is, to those who renounce their self-indulgence, self-confidence, and self-satisfaction. To all such Christ promises, "I will give [you] a place with me on my throne, just as I myself conquered and sat down with my Father on his throne" (3:21). The promise to rule with Christ is one that is made often (1:6; 5:10; 20:6; 22:5; see also Matthew 19:28; Luke 22:28-30; 2 Timothy 2:12). The symbolism of the throne signifies royal honor—and a place with Christ is the highest honor conceivable for a Christian.

In the final verse we hear for the seventh and last time the exhortation, "Listen to what the Spirit is saying to the churches" (3:22). It is noteworthy that although each oracle is addressed to a different church, the concluding formula always refers to "the churches." The message to each church is at the same time a message to all churches. The seven churches provide examples of the kinds of things that can go wrong in any church. These are: the danger of losing the love that one had at first (Ephesus), fear of suffering (Smyrna), doctrinal compromise (Pergamum), moral compromise (Thyatira), spiritual deadness (Sardis), failure to hold fast (Philadelphia), and lukewarmness (Laodicea). They also provide direction and incentive to the churches of every nation and age to overcome—to *conquer*—these challenges to faithfulness and triumph together in the Lamb.

5

JOHN'S VISION OF GOD AND THE LAMB

(Revelation 4:1–5:14)

While Revelation chapters 2 and 3 focus on the conditions of seven churches on earth (in western Asia Minor), chapters 4 and 5 focus on the activity of heaven. They describe John's vision of God on the throne and of the Lamb of God, who is, of course, Jesus Christ. Until now the symbols in Revelation have been relatively straightforward and their meaning relatively easy to understand. From here onward they become more difficult and complex. Nevertheless, by using a disciplined imagination, one can follow the author's meaning, at least to some degree.

John begins by saying that he saw a door standing open in heaven and heard a trumpet-like voice saying, "Come up here, and I will show you what must take place after this" (4:1).

On hearing the trumpet-like voice, John at once sensed that he "was in the spirit," an awareness continuing or corresponding to his experience referred to in 1:10, "I was in the spirit on the Lord's day." This enabled him to respond to the invitation, "Come up here," and to describe what he saw and heard after passing through the door opened in heaven. There he gazed on the majestic spectacle of a throne and of the Lord God Almighty seated on the throne (4:2). Here the New Revised Standard Version punctuates the sentence with an exclamation mark to suggest something of the profound awe that John experienced during his vision. In what follows he attempts to describe the transcendental glory and grandeur of God who reigns from the throne. But how was he to convey the dazzling brilliance of this exalted scene? John will frequently use the Greek words for "as" or "like" throughout his visions, signaling to his hearers that human language and experience cannot fully capture and communicate what he himself had seen and heard in the realm beyond. By means of these analogies, John invites his hearers to imaginatively engage his revelation, even as John himself had no doubt long engaged the visions of God enthroned in Isaiah 6 and Ezekiel 1, both of which deeply inform his own visionary experience and description thereof.

In accord with the reluctance of Jewish writers to picture God, John carefully avoids any descriptive detail. No form is visible, and the writer refrains from even mentioning the august name of God. He says that the one seated on the throne "looks like jasper and carnelian" (4:3). These are two precious or semiprecious stones. There are several kinds of what in ancient times was called jasper; probably John has in mind a translucent type of jasper, which is clear as crystal (see also 21:11). When such a stone is polished, it sparkles and flashes with luminous splendor—a beautiful and poetic way to describe visually what other biblical writers refer to as the holiness and glory of God.

In addition to jasper, John tells us that God looks like carnelian. This gemstone is usually a deep reddish color. When one holds a carnelian in one's hand, it seems as though a fire is smoldering inside the stone. Does John mean to suggest that, in addition to the holiness of God, God also burns in wrath against sin? If this is what is suggested, then John's conception of God is altogether like that of other biblical authors.

Continuing to contemplate the vision of God seated upon the throne, John notices that "around the throne is a rainbow that looks like an emerald" (4:3). It is popular to see here a reference to the sign of God's promise never again to destroy the earth by the waters of a flood (Genesis 9:11, 13), though the sign would be more ironic than reassuring given the manifold devastations of the earth that follow in the seven seals, trumpets, and bowls! The word rendered *rainbow* can also refer to a "halo," a bright circle of light. Indeed, John uses a word here that is *never* used in the Greek translation of the Old Testament to refer to the rainbow or God's covenant with Noah. It may be John's intent, therefore, to highlight the glory and splendor of the Almighty by referring to the radiant halo that encircles the throne, even as he will use the same image to highlight the glory of the great angel that will renew his own prophetic commission in 10:1. This is all the more likely as his restriction of the color to that of an emerald directs the hearers away from imagining an actual rainbow.

As John's gaze spreads out from the throne to the heavenly entourage, we encounter beings whose identity is not immediately clear to us. John is not the first, however, to describe God's throne and heavenly court, and the writings of earlier visionaries can be of some help to us here. The anonymous Jew who wrote Testament of

Levi, a text from around the turn of the era, takes on the persona of Levi, the third son of Jacob, and has an experience very similar to John's: "the heavens were opened, and an angel of the Lord spoke to me: 'Levi, Levi, enter!'" (Testament of Levi 2.6). Levi tours the seven heavens, the lowest three of which are gloomy, containing the elements reserved for judgment upon the earth. The upper four heavens are bright and glorious, all focused on God who sits upon a glorious throne in the uppermost heaven, in the "Holy of Holies" of the heavenly temple (Testament of Levi 3.4-5; 5.1). Levi also sees the various angelic orders, their actions conceived in terms of priestly and levitical duties.

John's description of God's heavenly entourage is quite in keeping with other such visions. John sees "twenty-four elders, dressed in white robes, with golden crowns on their heads" (Revelation 4:4), seated on thrones around God's throne. A number of interpreters have found a satisfactory explanation for these elders by identifying them as the twelve patriarchs of the Old Testament and the twelve apostles of the New Testament, symbolizing the two covenants of the people of God. John, however, may simply have been describing an order of angels he expected to find in God's entourage—the order known as "thrones" (Colossians 1:16). The awesome vision is enhanced by "flashes of lightning, and rumblings and peals of thunder" that issue from the throne (Revelation 4:5). One is reminded of similar visible and audible manifestations of God's presence on Sinai prior to giving the law to Moses (Exodus 19:16). In Hebrew poetry the thunderstorm suggests God's presence and majesty (1 Samuel 2:10). Again we see the seven flaming spirits, likely John's representation of the seven angels of the Presence known from Jewish tradition (Tobit 12:15; Testament of Levi 3.5-6).

Between John and the throne is a flat pavement-like surface, "like a sea of glass, like crystal" (4:6). The God of Israel had once seemed to stand on "something like a pavement of sapphire stone" (Exodus 24:10). John is probably alluding to this passage in Exodus and wishes to stress the magnificence of the throne and the distance still remaining between him and the throne. The description here could well have been linked to the expanse of the Aegean Sea viewed on a still, clear day from the hills of Patmos. The picture is one of immense distance and serenity.

John's description of the four living creatures on each side of the throne draws significantly upon Ezekiel's vision of God's chariot (Ezekiel 1:4-21), though John also supplies some of the features from Isaiah's vision of God enthroned in the temple (Isaiah 6:2). These are the cherubim—not at all like the chubby, winged infants advertising baby soap, but God's strong agents, representing power over all the created world. The four creatures in John's vision (4:7) have the appearance of a lion, an ox, a human being, and a flying eagle. These symbolize, respectively, what is the noblest, strongest, wisest, and swiftest in creation. Beginning with Irenaeus in the late second century, it became customary to associate these four figures with the four evangelists, generally the man with Matthew, the lion with Mark, the ox with Luke, and the eagle with John. Such association, which is entirely fanciful, has influenced many forms of Christian art.

The four living creatures, John says, are "full of eyes in front and behind" (4:6) and "full of eyes all around and inside" (4:8). The repeated phrase "full of eyes" suggests unsleeping watchfulness, as the creatures perceive everything in every direction. One should not attempt to picture these creatures literally; no diagram can show all these characteristics.

One function of the four living creatures, who are mentioned fourteen times in the book, is to act as choirmasters leading all the public worship in heaven constantly praising God, enthroned in majesty. "Whenever the living creatures give glory and honor and thanks" to the eternal one (4:9), the twenty-four elders prostrate themselves before the throne. In typical oriental fashion they lay down their crowns as a sign of their homage and as a dramatic demonstration of their acknowledgment of God's sovereignty. The crowns are God's gifts and are appropriately given back to God in worship.

The ceaseless worship of the four living creatures (4:8) does not imply that this worship is their sole activity, but rather that it is their constant disposition—their every action is an expression of adoration.

Joined by the twenty-four elders, the four living creatures give voice to two songs, probably examples of early congregational praise. One of the hymns, beginning "Holy, holy, holy" (4:8), celebrates the otherness of God, that is, the distinction between the Infinite and all finite beings. As in Isaiah's vision of "the Lord sitting on a throne, high and lofty" (Isaiah 6:1-3), the threefold repetition of "holy" designates the superlative degree. God alone is the holiest, most powerful, and everlasting one. The second hymn praises God as creator: "You are worthy, our Lord and God, to receive glory and honor and power, for you created all things, and by your will they existed and were created" (Revelation 4:11). Here the twenty-four elders ascribe to the Creator the name that the emperor Domitian had usurped, "our Lord and God" (see p. 21). As the Giver of life and breath to all that exist, God alone merits worship as an expression of the deepest gratitude and obeisance.

Such descriptions of the enthroned God and his praise would come as a tonic to persecuted Christians and a warning to those tempted to collude and compromise. John's vision reminded them of the splendor and majesty and power of God that outstrip all the pretensions of the human emperors and pagan deities, the enthroned counterfeits in Rome and in their temples across the Mediterranean.

The account of John's vision continues in chapter 5, when John's attention is drawn to a scroll that is held in the right hand of the one seated upon the throne. Written on the inside and on the back, it was sealed with seven seals (5:1). The scroll's contents will only become clear as it begins to be opened in chapter 6. For now, the seven seals indicate that its contents are completely hidden, so that "no one in heaven or on earth or under the earth was able to open the scroll or to look into it" (5:3).

John began to weep bitterly because no one could be found who was worthy to open the scroll and, thus, to advance God's plan for human history. Then one of the elders said, "Do not weep. See, the Lion of the tribe of Judah, the Root of David, has conquered, so that he can open the scroll and its seven seals" (5:5). The expressions "Lion of the tribe of Judah" and "Root of David" are scriptural references (Genesis 49:9; Isaiah 11:1, 10) pointing to the coming Messiah.

What follows is altogether unexpected. John looked to see the Lion, the king of beasts, and instead he sees a Lamb with the marks of slaughter upon it (5:6)! He looked to see power and force, by which the enemies of his faith would be destroyed, and he sees sacrificial love and meek obedience to God as the way to win the victory. Most Jews had been expecting a Messiah who would break the yoke of the Roman imperial power and liberate his people by violent revolution. The might of the Messiah God sent, however, is the power of self-giving love. The poetic symbolism of the author is heightened still further when the Lamb is described as having seven horns and seven eyes. This should not be taken as a literal description. Rather, the seven horns mean that Christ has complete power, and the seven eyes mean that he sees and knows all things. Compare the repeated "I know . . . " at the opening of each of the seven letters of the churches in chapters 2 and 3, as well as the penetrating gaze of him whose eyes are like a flame of fire (1:14; 2:18; 19:12).

The fundamental transformation of the messianic expectation became obvious on that first Palm Sunday when Jesus presented himself as God's Messiah. He rode into Jerusalem, not on a warhorse, equipped with all kinds of armor, but on a donkey, a symbol of peace and humility. Instead of a ferocious lion that hurts others, the Messiah is a sacrificial lamb that takes into himself the hurts of others. According to Isaiah 53:5, which has colored the Christian understanding of the mission of Jesus, "He was wounded for our transgressions, crushed for our iniquities; . . . and by his bruises we are healed."

The Lamb—not a literal four-hoofed creature, but the visionary description of Jesus—is alone able to carry out God's commission to enact his final decrees for human history, and so he "took the scroll from the right hand of the one who was seated on the throne" (5:7). In opening the scroll, the Lamb is about to disclose what the scroll contains. In short, Jesus does not change the divine plan; he unfolds its eternal and unchangeable nature by his obedience, even unto death on the cross. There is an also implicit claim being made for Jesus here: he possesses a divine dignity and authority that far outstrips the dignity and authority of any rival, including the Roman emperors who were *not* worthy to step into that silence in heaven and take the scroll from God's right hand.

No wonder there is praise in heaven, accompanied by incense and harps. The twenty-four elders fall before the Lamb and offer "golden bowls full of incense, which are the prayers of the saints" (5:8). Here is John's first hint of the participation of the church's worship on earth with that of the church in heaven. This idea appears also near the close of the Apostles' Creed, when Christians confess that they believe in "the communion of saints." This communion of saints is not just the fellowship we enjoy with other people during a service of worship, but it includes also the idea that John expresses here—the unity of worship of the church embattled on earth with that of the church triumphant in heaven. The prayers of believers here on earth are mingled with the worship of angels and archangels and all the host of heaven, in adoration of God and the Lamb.

In words that recollect the praise offered to God for having created all things (4:11), so now a new song is sung in praise of the Lamb: "You are worthy to take the scroll and to open its seals, for you were slaughtered and by your blood you ransomed for God saints from every tribe and language and people and nation" (5:9). Here there is a hint that just as the Passover lamb's blood protected the firstborn of the Israelites from the plague of death, so too "the Lamb of God who takes away the sin of the world" (John 1:29) will protect the faithful from the wrath to come. Just as all people owe the enthroned God a life-debt for their existence, so all owe the Lamb a life-debt for their redemption! Suddenly the power of the scene and the song is picked up by an innumerable host of angels, numbering "myriads of myriads and thousands of thousands" (5:11). Mathematically this works out to one hundred million plus one million, but probably John simply means an infinite number. The angels repeat three of the elders' terms of praise: glory, honor, and power, and add wealth, wisdom, might, and blessing (5:12). The seven terms symbolize the fullness of the praise. Then, with thrilling crescendo, all creation joins in adoration and praise to God and to the Lamb. The chapter concludes with a great "Amen!" as the elders fall down in worship.

And so, with these glorious affirmations of the goodness and mercy of God Almighty and of the Lamb ringing in John's ears, he can endure with confidence, despite the terrors about to be let loose on the world described in the following chapters. John's vision will have a profound effect on his hearers. The Christians are a small minority group worshiping behind closed doors in the corners of their cities. Around them, tens of thousands pay open homage to the traditional gods and the emperors' images. But the Christians are not the deviant ones—they join their voices "with angels and archangels and all the company of heaven"[1] to worship the true center of the cosmos, as God's forthcoming interventions will make clear to all.

6

OPENING THE SEVEN SEALS OF GOD'S SCROLL

(Revelation 6:1–8:5)

With the sixth chapter, the main action of the book may be said properly to begin. The section extending from Revelation chapter 6 to the end of chapter 16 is intended to bring before the reader not only the struggle of the church amid conflict and persecution but also the judgments of God upon the church's enemies.

We should note the outline that John follows through these eleven chapters. The first section is dramatically arranged in a series of seven scenes that are revealed as the Lamb opens each of the seven seals. The first four seals will be opened at once and will together make up one picture. Then the fifth and sixth seals will be opened, together making up one picture. Some intermediate material leads finally to the opening of the seventh seal. The seventh seal, in turn, introduces a new series of visions, announced by the blowing of seven trumpets in turn. Again the same outline is followed. First, four trumpets will be sounded, making one unified impression. Then the fifth and sixth trumpets, together giving one impression. After this, another series of intermediate visions, leading finally to the last of the trumpets, which gives way to more visions and, eventually, the pouring out of the seven bowls, with which "the wrath of God is ended" (15:1).

This complicated and repetitious pattern gives a sense of unity and inexorable, forward progression to John's visions, interlocking the various parts and at the same time developing his themes. The progression, however, does not move in a strictly linear fashion, such as we are familiar with in Western narrative, but rather brings "the end" before us again and again, keeping it ever in view (6:12-16; 11:15-18; 14:14-20; 19:11–20:15).

The first four seals (6:1-8) are unified by their common image, the vision of the four horsemen of the Apocalypse. The description of this vision has features borrowed from Zechariah 6:1-5, which also involves horses of various colors—red, black, white, dappled gray. The Apocalyptist, however, borrows only the symbol of the horses and their colors, and instead of yoking the horses to chariots he sets on each of them a rider in whom the interest of the vision is centered.

The vision of the four horsemen begins when the Lamb, who has already taken the scroll from God's right hand (5:7), begins to open its seven seals one by one. The first four events are marked by common features. Each is preceded by an utterance from one of the four living creatures and followed by the appearance of a horse and its rider, whose significance is partly explained. But there are also many puzzling aspects. John says:

I saw the Lamb open one of the seven seals, and I heard one of the four living creatures call out, as with a voice of thunder, "Come!" I looked, and there was a white horse! Its rider had a bow; a crown was given to him, and he came out conquering and to conquer.

When he opened the second seal, I heard the second living creature call out, "Come!" And out came another horse, bright red; its rider was permitted to take peace from the earth, so that people would slaughter one another; and he was given a great sword.

When he opened the third seal, I heard the third living creature call out, "Come!" I looked, and there was a black horse! Its rider held a pair of scales in his hand, and I heard what seemed to be a voice in the midst of the four living creatures saying, "A quart of wheat for a day's pay, and three quarts of barley for a day's pay, but do not damage the olive oil and the wine!"

When he opened the fourth seal, I heard the voice of the fourth living creature call out, "Come!" I looked and there was a pale green horse! Its rider's name was Death, and Hades followed with him; they were given authority over a fourth of the earth, to kill with sword, famine, and pestilence, and by the wild animals of the earth.

(6:1-8)

The accounts are brief and concise. Each of the four scenes is like a cameo, very small and compact. None of the four horsemen says a single word. Each rides forth in silence. We do not know in which direction they ride, because the Greek word translated "Come!" may also be translated "Go!" Do they ride from heaven to earth, or from one place on earth to another place on earth? What is the significance of this vision of the four horsemen?

One of the features that distinguishes the Book of Revelation from other books of the New Testament is the author's attempt to show how power fits into the divine scheme of things. John begins with the belief that all power comes from God. God is the absolute ruler of the world. But because God gave humankind free will, there is always the possibility that we might misuse the portion of power entrusted to us. When this happens, however, it does not mean that God is helpless and frustrated. The world is still God's world and is still ruled in accordance with the eternal laws of right and wrong. One of those laws is that human misuse of power brings on suffering and disaster. Wars, starvation, devastation—these make plain that power abused is still under God's control. These are the "judgments" of God, being worked out on the plane of history.

Bearing this in mind, we can approach more sympathetically this chapter with its succession of terrible calamities. First, there is the white horse. Its rider holds a bow and he rides off on a career of conquest. The key to the meaning may lie in the bow, which was the characteristic weapon of the mounted Parthian warriors. Parthia was a formidable neighbor on the eastern border of the Roman Empire, and Parthian invasion a much-feared possibility. The white horse may conjure up the impression of a Parthian invasion that meets with success. But the bow was also the weapon of Apollo, the patron god of Domitian, and of Artemis/Diana, another prominent deity in the pantheon, and Roman armies had their archery divisions. Going forth "conquering and to conquer" was what Rome was known for. John may see in this first horseman Rome's own violent expansion of its empire, which brings the following evils in its train.

When the second seal is opened, there appears a red horse. Its rider holds a huge sword, and he is "permitted to take peace from the earth, so that people would slaughter one another" (6:4). This obviously symbolizes war and bloodshed. The removal of "peace" may represent a stab at the "Roman peace" much celebrated by the emperors, but shattered in recent history by their own grabs for power in the devastating civil wars of AD 68–69.

The third horse is black; its rider holds a pair of scales, and John hears a voice saying, "A quart of wheat for a day's pay, and three quarts of barley for a day's pay, but do not damage the olive oil and the wine!" (6:6). Usually a day's pay (a denarius) could purchase eight to sixteen times more grain than the amounts mentioned here. In other words, imperial expansion and civil war are followed by inflation and famine. There is an echo here of conditions in Roman Asia specifically under Domitian, for the large landholders had converted more and more of their arable land to vineyards and olive groves so as to reap more of the profits of international trade in these costlier products, diminishing the supply of grain and inflating its prices beyond the reach of the common person.

The fourth horseman is Death, riding a horse the color of decaying flesh. Hades, the place of the dead, follows close behind. We have here all the appalling aftermath of war—famine, pestilence, and the final devastation when wild animals overrun what was once the habitat of people (6:8).

These disasters are the results of the working out of God's righteous laws for the universe. God does not approve of famine and death and hell, but they are what must follow if people persist in opposing God's rule. God wills community, which is the consequence of caring and love. Ignore physical laws, like stepping off a cliff, and disaster follows. Neglect moral laws, and disaster ensues just as surely. The woes described here are the result of not taking seriously God's command to achieve community and justice. God does not will the woes, but as long as we are free agents, God allows them. The four horsemen of the Apocalypse are brilliant little vignettes that show what happens in the sphere of politics, of military action, and of economics whenever men and women oppose the will of God. There are few chapters in Revelation that speak more directly to our time than this part of chapter 6. In books, in newspapers, in magazine articles, in radio and television broadcasts, and in various social media, we read and hear about the four horsemen of the Apocalypse, who continue their gallop across the earth today. We hear the cry for justice; we sense that there must be a judgment in which the guilty will not be able to escape.

With the opening of the fifth seal, the action shifts from earth to heaven (6:9-11). During the scene of heavenly worship, we saw the twenty-four elders holding golden bowls of incense, identified as the prayers of the saints (5:8). Now as the Lamb breaks the fifth seal, we learn more about these desperate prayers as we see the souls of these martyred Christians under the altar in the heavenly temple, crying out for justice against those who had shed their blood. They are told, however, that they must wait until God's appointed time; persecution must first fully run its course (6:11), as our sisters and brothers across the globe daily experience, their cries also ascending to heaven. Then all those who have suffered on Christ's account will be vindicated together. Meanwhile, the martyrs can already enjoy their rightful place in heaven; they were each given their white robe of purity, victory, and service (6:11).

With the breaking of the sixth seal by the Lamb, God's punishments of the wicked are resumed (6:12-17). In his description of these, John makes use of symbolism drawn from many parts of the Old Testament: the earthquake from Haggai (2:6), the sun turned black and the moon turned to blood from Joel (2:31), the stars fallen from heaven like figs from a fig tree (Isaiah 34:4), and the sky rolled up like a scroll (Isaiah 34:4). The use of cosmic convulsions to describe social and political upheaval is well established in biblical prophecy (compare the picture of chaos in Jeremiah 4:23-26, where the desolation caused by foreign invaders is intended). Precisely what is denoted by the details of this highly colorful language is difficult to determine. In any case, John clearly describes the terror of an impenitent world. All classes of society, from the potentates and generals of Rome to "everyone, slave and free" (Revelation 6:15), are thrust into abject terror and dread before the appearance of the just and holy God and his Messiah. John has catapulted us forward to the Day of the Lord, the "great day of their wrath" (6:17), when God will have satisfaction for his creatures' refusal to acknowledge the one God and God's Anointed, persisting instead in their idolatries and their neglect of their Creator's commandments. Their rhetorical question—"who is able to stand?"—is important to hold in mind, for John will answer it in the next chapter.

Between the opening of the sixth and seventh seals, there is an interlude of two consolatory visions (7:1-8 and 7:9-17). These provide assurance that God's people are secure from the plagues and judgments. Four angels at the four corners of the earth hold back the winds of judgment, causing a temporary suspension of the plagues (7:1) until God's elect are marked with a seal (7:2-3).

John then sees another angel flying from the east bearing "the seal of the living God" (7:2). He hears of 144,000 people, 12,000 from each of the twelve tribes of Israel, receiving God's stamp upon their foreheads.[1] The idea of a ruler's seal would be familiar. Eastern kings and Roman emperors both sealed documents with signet rings to authenticate them and to mark personal property. So when the 144,000 were sealed (7:2-4), the seal signifies that they belonged to God and were under God's power and protection. While they are still subject to the violence of human beings (as the two witnesses in Revelation chapter 11 will be killed by the beast), they are exempted from suffering God's judgments, even as the plagues God sent upon Egypt did not fall upon the Hebrews of old. Furthermore, the explicit number, 144,000, symbolizes completeness—not one of the redeemed is missing.

Next, John sees an innumerable multitude standing before the throne and before the Lamb (7:9-17). They are robed in white and are carrying palm branches, denoting that they are victors.

One of the elders identifies the multitude clad in white as those "who have come out of the great ordeal; they have washed their robes and made them white in the blood of the Lamb" (7:14). These words, taken literally, are paradoxical; washing a garment in blood does not make it white. On the other hand, the words do convey the symbolism that is consistent throughout the New Testament. It is a vivid way of saying that their present blessedness and their fitness to appear in the presence of God have been won for them by the sacrificial death of Christ. While the benefits of redemption are provided by Christ, the redeemed also have their part to play; they "washed their robes." What John conveys to us here with startling symbolism is expressed by the apostle Paul in more prosaic language: "Work out your own salvation with fear and trembling; for it is God who is at work in you, enabling you both to will and to work for his good pleasure" (Philippians 2:12-13).

Revelation chapter 7 ends with words that have brought comfort and consolation to millions. There are no words more comforting in the ears of those who have been bereaved than the closing promise:

"They will hunger no more, and thirst no more;
the sun will not strike them,
nor any scorching heat;
for the Lamb at the center of the throne will be their
shepherd,
and he will guide them to springs of the water
of life,
and God will wipe away every tear from their eyes."

(7:16-17)

The precise relationship between these two groups in 7:4-8 and 7:9-17 remains a mystery. John only *sees* the second group, having *heard* about the first group, so that it is possible that these refer to the same group—the initial expectations for the group (a remnant of Israel) yielding to the larger reality (the redeemed from every nation), much like the "Lion of the tribe of Judah" was revealed to be the slaughtered Lamb (5:5-6). Another possible relationship may be seen in the location of each group. The 144,000 on earth are being sealed in preparation for the judgments God is about to unleash upon the inhabitants of the earth and will stand beside the Lamb in his combat against the Beast (14:1-5); the innumerable multitude enjoy their eternal triumph in the presence and shelter of the God and Messiah they served. We may, then, have a vision of the Church Embattled and the Church Triumphant, the second vision encouraging those who continue in the thick of the strife.

Those familiar with medieval art have seen diptychs, two paintings on two separate pieces of wood connected by a hinge. These paintings are intended to be seen and pondered together, to be mutually reinforcing or mutually interpreting. John often presents verbal diptychs in his Revelation, one of which is seen in these chapters. In 6:12-17 John depicts the abject terror with which the unfaithful and disobedient will encounter God and his

Christ on that great Day; in 7:9-17, John depicts those who *will* be able to "stand" before God and the Lamb—those who have been faithful in their obedience and their witness in the midst of the challenges of this life. The twin portraits pose an implicit question to John's hearers and readers in every age: How do you wish to encounter God and the Lamb on that great Day? How does your answer to this question illumine the choices and challenges you must face today?

The sequence of the opening of the seven seals is now resumed: one more seal is to be opened, the last. We might have expected this to end the drama and introduce the final cataclysm. But nothing happens. Instead, "there was silence in heaven for about half an hour" (8:1). It is like the solemn hush before the bursting of a hurricane. The pause heightens the solemnity and horror of the next series of God's judgments, each to be announced by the sounding of a trumpet. However, this silence in heaven is more than a dramatic interlude. Rather, it creates the space for a liturgical act in heaven of great significance. An angel approaches the heavenly altar with a censer full of incense, the smoke of which rose before God "with the prayers of all the saints" (8:3). He then fills the censer with the burning coals from the altar and casts the fiery implement upon the earth. The import of these symbolic actions is straightforward, assuring John's congregations that their prayers are indeed heard in heaven *and* will prove effectual on earth. This vision continues to encourage particularly our persecuted sisters and brothers throughout the world that God hears their cries and *will* give justice for them against their oppressors.

7

SOUNDING THE SEVEN TRUMPETS

(Revelation 8:6–11:19)

In these next scenes, seven angels blow their trumpets one after another, announcing hailstorms with fire and blood descending, volcanic eruptions, blood in the sea, blight on the land, the pollution of springs and fountains, eclipses of sun and moon with shooting stars, climaxed by plagues of demonic locusts and cavalry.

These seven angels are identified as "the seven angels who stand before God" (8:2), the seven who, according to Jewish tradition, formed an elite order of archangels. In Tobit, a Jewish text written during the intertestamental period, an angel reveals himself thus: "I am Raphael, one of the seven angels who stand ready and enter before the glory of the Lord" (Tobit 12:15). The names of the other six, according to the Greek text of 1 Enoch (20:1-7), are Uriel, Raguel, Michael, Sariel, Gabriel, and Remiel. It is to these angels that John sees seven trumpets being given, which will summon the following judgments. The trumpet is the favorite instrument of apocalyptists since its strident tones historically summoned the people's attention to God's communications and presence.

Like the opening of the seven seals (Revelation 6:1–8:1), the sounding of the seven trumpets falls into two groups of four and three. John's description of the series of God's judgments recalls and reconfigures the ten plagues sent against the Egyptians to persuade Pharaoh to let the people of Israel go (Exodus 7–12). John suggests that Rome is not the bringer of prosperity and peace, but a new oppressive power like Egypt, from which Christians should seek liberation rather than partnership.

The last of the four horsemen had authority to harm a fourth of the earth (6:8). At the sounding of the first trumpet the destruction becomes more pervasive, for now one-third is affected (8:7). With the second, third, and fourth trumpets there is a continuation of the affliction of the earth in terms of one-third: sea, sea creatures, ships, rivers, fountains of water, sun, moon, stars.

The imagery that John uses to describe his visions may have been in part suggested by storms, earthquakes, and eclipses of the first century. If, as is likely, Revelation was written after AD 79, when the sudden eruption of Vesuvius completely engulfed the cities of Pompeii and Herculaneum with molten lava and destroyed ships in the Gulf of Naples, then John's readers, having heard reports of the catastrophe, would have had no difficulty picturing "something like a great mountain, burning with fire, [being] thrown into the sea" (8:8).

SOUNDING THE SEVEN TRUMPETS

The judgments that follow each of the first four trumpets are elemental forces of nature, which are directed against the cosmos and which affect humanity indirectly. The last three trumpets call forth demonic forces, falling directly on humanity. These are introduced by an eagle, circling high in midheaven and crying out, "Woe, woe, woe to the inhabitants of the earth, at the blasts of the other trumpets that the three angels are about to blow!" (8:13). This announcement of foreboding warns the reader that worse things are to follow.

As in the sequence of the seals, so in the sequence of the trumpets the fifth and sixth are described at greater length than the first four. When the fifth angel blows his trumpet, a plague of demonic locusts is released from the bottomless pit (9:3). The leader of these demonic hordes is Abaddon, the "destroyer." Lest the reader fail to grasp the significance of the Hebrew name, John adds the Greek equivalent, Apollyon (9:11). John's vision may represent a subversive satire of imperial ideology. Domitian claimed Apollo, one of whose symbols was the locust, as his patron deity; in John's cosmos, however, "Apollo" is a creature of the abyss, the chief of a horde of demonic locusts. Unlike any natural swarm of locusts, these are like cavalry horses armed for battle. They have human faces, they wear gold crowns, their hair is like women's hair, their teeth are like lions' teeth, and they have tails with poisonous stings like scorpions (9:7-10). The vividness of John's description is not meant to provide individual details to be interpreted, but to create a vivid impression on the hearers' imaginations and to evoke thereby a visceral response of fear for the fate that awaits those who have denied the one God.

The mission of these demonic tormentors is not to harm the vegetation on earth, as natural locusts would (9:4). Their attack is to be launched against all who have denied their Creator, who therefore lack his seal, for a period of five months (9:5), the usual life cycle of certain species of natural locusts. Just as the Israelites had been exempt from the plagues of Egypt, so now the Christians who have God's seal upon their foreheads will be completely unharmed by these awful creatures of divine judgment (9:4). So great will be the suffering caused by the locusts that people prefer death to the agony of living. But death will elude them (9:6).

Then the sixth angel blows his trumpet (9:13) and summons a vast host of unnatural cavalry, two hundred million in number, to cross the Euphrates River and to kill a third of humankind. The Euphrates is significant as the eastern frontier of the Roman Empire, beyond which lay the Parthian menace. These demon-horsemen with their mounts, hitherto held in leash, are now let loose like avenging furies upon the Roman provinces at "the hour, the day, the month, and the year" appointed (9:15). The horses of the invaders are frightful, supernatural agents of destruction. They kill people by the fire, smoke, and sulfur issuing from their mouths, and poison them by their tails, which are like the heads of serpents (9:17-19). The author of Wisdom of Solomon, a Greek-speaking Jew writing around the turn of the era, contemplated God's restraint when punishing the Egyptians: "For your all-powerful hand, which created the world out of formless matter, did not lack the means to send upon them a multitude of bears, or bold lions, or newly-created unknown beasts full of rage, or such as breathe out fiery breath, or belch forth a thick pall of smoke, or flash terrible sparks from their eyes; not only could the harm they did destroy people, but the mere sight of them could kill by fright" (Wisdom of Solomon 11:17-19, Apocrypha). In this greater, universal Exodus, however, the gloves have come off!

We must remember that the objects and events seen in a vision are not physically real. As was mentioned earlier (see pp. 16–17),

Ezekiel's vision of the valley of dry bones (Ezekiel 37) and Peter's vision of a great sheet let down from heaven and filled with all kinds of unclean creatures (Acts 10) were perceived in a trance. Such things seen in a vision are not physically present. So too, in the Book of Revelation, the descriptions are not descriptions of real occurrences, but of symbols of the real occurrences. The intention is to fix the reader's thought, not upon the symbol, but upon the idea that the symbolic language is designed to convey.

Dire though the imagery is, the underlying purpose of these judgments is not to inflict vengeance but to drive people to repentance. Although nothing is done to minimize the gravity of sin and rebellion against God, there is great emphasis on God's patience and mercy. Instead of total destruction, only a third (9:18) or some other fraction of the whole is affected. The fraction is symbolic of the mercy of God. The calamity is not yet universal but leaves those who can learn from tragic events. The seven trumpets stand hereby in contrast to the seven bowls to follow, with which God's anger is completed and finally poured out (15:1).

It would be natural to think that the remainder of humanity would have taken warning from such dreadful portents. But they do not; they brazenly refuse all opportunity to turn back to God (9:20-21). It is because of their continued stubbornness that pressure on the wicked is progressively increased. With a keen eye to the basic wrong in human nature, John identifies the sin to which the survivors cling so tenaciously: idolatry. For John this involved emperor worship alongside the worship of the traditional Greco-Roman gods that were everywhere present in the seven cities. Whatever its form in that age or in any other age, however, the worship of anyone or anything but God alone is always the greatest evil and the parent of all evils (see the list in 9:20-21; also Romans 1:18-32).

Between the sounding of the sixth and seventh trumpets there is another pause (10:1–11:14), just as there was an interlude before the breaking of the seventh seal. The visions that make up this interlude, however, describe the mingling of the sweet and the bitter. They speak of persecution and tribulation, but also of loyalty and devotion, particularly as exemplified in bold proclamation (chapter 10) and witness (chapter 11).

These interludes admittedly heighten the drama, as we hold our breath in anticipation of the seventh event in each series. But the interludes also convey essential information and pose foundational challenges to the hearers. In this interlude, John's prophetic commission is renewed, reminding his hearers of his divinely-given authority (chapter 10), and the Christian ideal—the empowered, undaunted witness to God and his Messiah—is presented (chapter 11).

John sees "another mighty angel coming down from heaven, wrapped in a cloud, with a rainbow [or radiant halo] over his head" (10:1). When this angel speaks, seven thunders speak. Yet another entire cycle of seven is thrown on the screen momentarily and then removed after only a glance has been permitted. The effect is tantalizing. This cycle of seven thunders was clearly witnessed by the writer, and he was about to write what he had heard when he was told, "Seal up what the seven thunders have said, and do not write it down" (10:4). The effect of this strange aside is to subtly remind John's audience that, despite his readiness and willingness to reveal all that he has seen and heard, he knows more than he can reveal—a fact that can only enhance his authority among the congregations (compare the use to which Paul puts his revelation of things that cannot be revealed in 2 Corinthians 12:1-10!).

The angel is holding a little scroll open in his hand, and John is told to "take it, and eat" (Revelation 10:9)—a way of saying that he is to "read, learn, mark, and inwardly digest," even as we still speak of "devouring a book," meaning that we read it with eagerness. This scroll, now unrolled and thus "open," cannot help but recall the sealed scroll whose seals the Lamb had broken and, thus, would now stand open. This device contributes to the unity of John's visions as we will now learn the remainder of that scroll's message in John's continued witness. The commissioning scene here is patterned after Ezekiel's own commission, in which he was given a scroll to eat by an angel, a scroll that proved sweet as honey in his mouth. John's prophetic message, however, is decidedly more mixed: while it will be sweet as honey in his mouth, it will turn his stomach (10:10), signifying that it is sweet to him to receive God's message, but that its wrath and judgment fill him with sorrow. Having assimilated the contents of the little scroll, John is commanded to make them known by prophesying "about many peoples and nations and languages and kings" (10:11).

What follows in Revelation chapter 11 is one of the most perplexing sections of the entire book—a bewildering interweaving of symbols from Old Testament history and prophecy. We find references to the temple and the altar, to Moses and Elijah, to the wild olive trees and the lampstand seen by Zechariah, to the plagues sent upon Pharaoh, to the tyrant predicted by Daniel, and to Sodom and Egypt and Jerusalem. The general import of the chapter is clear: the author views the people of God as bearing faithful testimony, but also as suffering pain and persecution and indignity. They are delivered not *from* martyrdom and death, but *through* martyrdom and death to a glorious resurrection. Nevertheless, beyond such a very general understanding of the passage, some features of Revelation 11:1-14 can be clarified by the patient expositor who seeks to discriminate between what is to be understood literally and what is to be understood symbolically.

How should we take John's statement when he says that he was given a measuring rod and told to "measure the temple of God and the altar and those who worship there" (11:1)? This certainly cannot refer to the Jewish temple in Jerusalem, for when John is writing in the 90s it had been lying in ruins for some twenty years after the Roman armies under Titus had devastated the city in AD 70. John may subscribe to the idea that the desert tabernacle and the Jerusalem temple were models of the cosmos (see Josephus, *The Antiquities of the Jews* 3.6.4 §§122-23; 3.7.7 §§180-81; Philo, *The Special Laws* 1.66). We have already encountered the accoutrements of the holy places and inner courts in John's heaven (Revelation 6:9; 8:3-5) and will again (11:19; 15:5-8; 16:7). If John's view of the cosmos was at all similar to that of Philo or Josephus, the inhabited earth would correlate to the outer courts of Israel and the Gentile nations. "Measuring" is a symbol for protection and preservation: the saints who have already passed from earth to God's realm, including those already martyred, are protected. They enjoy asylum, as it were, in God's own sanctuary. John is commanded, however, *not* to "measure the court outside the temple…for it is given over to the nations" (11:2). Those who remain in the world must endure the rampages of the nations in their revolt against God and God's saints, and it is onto such a field that God's witnesses must bravely step.

The aggressors have authority only "for forty-two months." This period is also the equivalent of three and a half years and 1,260 days, a term limit that is often assigned to the raging of an oppressor. It is derived from Daniel 9:27 and 12:7, where its primary reference is to the time of defilement of the temple by the "abomination that desolates" set up by Antiochus IV from 167 to 164 BC. It is during this term, and under these conditions, that the two witnesses exercise their ministry (11:3). Who are these two witnesses? John creates a composite picture that combines "the two olive trees" (11:4) of Zechariah's vision, by which the prophet meant the priestly Joshua and kingly Zerubbabel (Zechariah 4:1-14), with the activity of Elijah and Moses, who "shut the sky, so that no rain may fall" and turned water into blood (Revelation 11:6; 2 Kings 1:10; Exodus 7:17, 19).

When the two witnesses "have finished their testimony," they are attacked and killed by the beast from the bottomless pit (Revelation 11:7; see Revelation chapters 13 and 17). Their witness and martyrdom take place in "the great city," which is elsewhere identified with Rome (16:19; 17:18). Here it is linked to every city distinguished for its opposition to God: Sodom, which was possessed of such moral degradation that God selected it for extinction (Genesis 19:4-11); Egypt, the house of bondage (Exodus 20:2); and Jerusalem, where Christ was crucified (Revelation 11:8). The bodies of the witnesses "lie in the street of the great city . . . for three and a half days" (11:8-9). To deny proper burial was considered a great disgrace and insult to the dead.

Members from all "peoples and tribes and languages and nations" (11:9) celebrate because the two prophets are dead and can no longer vex their conscience by calling them to repentance. But God intervenes amid their gloating, gives his servants resurrection-life, and calls them up to heaven (11:11-12). The grim aftermath following the assumption of God's witnesses is the judgment of God on the wicked city that killed them (11:13). A destructive earthquake wrecks a tenth of the city and brings death to seven thousand of its inhabitants. Shocked out of their lethargy, those who survive are terrified and give glory to the God of heaven (11:13). How often the blood of martyrs becomes the seed of the church! (Tertullian).

What John is concerned to bring out in this section is that the church, whose lot it is to suffer the persecution of this world, will nevertheless continue to give faithful witness to the truth. Indeed, while plagues do not produce repentance, the faithful witness of God's servants does. The identity of the two witnesses remains murky, perhaps precisely because John wants his hearers to aspire to *be* such witnesses in their settings and to move boldly into that role assured of two things: God will empower their witness for precisely as long as God desires; God will vindicate God's faithful witnesses in the sight of their persecutors. The last word on their lives will not be the shame and degradation imposed by a hostile society, but the honor that God will grant in bestowing life beyond death and a place of distinction in God's kingdom.

This section of the Book of Revelation closes with the sounding of the last of the seven trumpets (11:15). What startles us is that what follows is so utterly unlike anything that the other trumpets announced. It is quite unique that here, instead of such things as volcanic eruptions, demonic locusts, and fire-breathing monsters, we listen to an outburst of rejoicing in heaven. John hears the heavenly chorus celebrating victory: "The kingdom of the world has become the kingdom of our Lord and of his Messiah, and he will reign forever and ever" (11:15).

Following this outburst of praise there comes a response from the twenty-four elders. They celebrate God's assumption of power, his overthrow of the raging nations, his judgment of the dead, and his rewarding of the faithful (11:16-18). Suddenly the song sinks into silence and there bursts on John's sight a new vision of divine glory: "God's temple in heaven was opened" (11:19), revealing the ark of the covenant, the sign of God's presence with his people. The outcome of all the judgments, the essence of all the rewards, is to have a more perfect access to God and a clearer vision of his splendor.

Certainly this has all the appearance of the end of the age, with the judging of those who have ravaged the earth's resources and victimized its populations, and rewarding of the saints and all who fear God's name, both small and great (11:18). If John had finished his book here, we would have considered it properly terminated. But since there are eleven more chapters, the author will now go back to an earlier stage and repeat some of the teachings that he had previously set before the reader. Thus, we see once again that the sequence in which John's visions are presented does not allow us to turn the Book of Revelation into an almanac or time chart of the last days.

8

THE SATANIC COUNTERFEIT: THE DRAGON AND THE TWO BEASTS

(Revelation 12:1–14:5)

Chapter 11 of the Book of Revelation concludes with references to judging the dead, rewarding the servants of God, and opening God's temple in heaven. Although this scenario would make a fitting end of the book, John has still more to reveal to the reader. To present this further material, he returns to an earlier stage and, so to speak, begins all over again. Chapter 12 can be characterized as a flashback, telling of the birth of the Messiah and the attempt of King Herod to kill Jesus soon after he was born. However, instead of telling this as a historical narrative in a straightforward manner as Matthew does (Matthew 2), John presents a heavenly tableau of characters portrayed with sensational Near Eastern imagery. John borrows old mythic motifs as he paints this picture. Striking parallels to the story of a celestial woman who together with her child is threatened by a great serpentine monster have been found in Babylonian, Persian, Egyptian, and Greek mythology and in astrological lore. One particularly close background is the story of Leto, who gives birth to the twin gods Apollo and Artemis, and who must save them from the dreaded Python that seeks to kill them. The more important question, however, is not what sources John may have used, but what use he now makes of them.

John opens his account with a graphic description of a great portent in heaven. The word *portent,* which occurs here for the first time in his book, marks the beginning of a new series of visions. John sees "a woman clothed with the sun, with the moon under her feet, and on her head a crown of twelve stars" (12:1). She is about to give birth to a child. Meanwhile John's attention is drawn to another great but ominous portent in heaven: "a great red dragon, with seven heads and ten horns" (12:3). Everyone knows that a dragon is fearful enough, but this is a great red dragon! His huge size is suggested by the comment that, while crouching in the sky, a flick of his tail dislodges a third of the stars and sends them hurtling to earth. Then the dragon stands before the woman in order to devour her child as soon as it is born. The woman bears a son, but the child is saved from the dragon by God's intervention.

What does all this signify? John himself tells us in verse 9 that the dragon represents Satan, the devil. Furthermore, the child is obviously the Christ, for again John provides the key by identifying him as the one "who is to rule all the nations with a rod of iron" (12:5). These words, taken from Psalm 2:9, were understood by Jews as a prediction of the role of the coming Messiah. The dragon's eagerness to devour the child explains the violent opposition that Jesus met during his earthly ministry. It began with the slaughter of the children in Bethlehem (Matthew 2:16) and culminated when he was crucified outside the city of Jerusalem.

Satan, however, is thwarted. The child is "snatched away and taken to God and to his throne" (12:5)—a reference to the Ascension. Here the gospel story is surprisingly condensed, but enough is said to accomplish John's purpose. He has shown the deadly enmity of the adversary, his defeat, and the exaltation of Christ to the place of supreme and universal power.

The woman, clothed with the sun, standing on the moon, and wearing a crown of stars, has been variously interpreted by some as the Virgin Mary, by others as the Christian church, and by still others as the Jewish people. What John probably intended was a personification of the community of God's people, first in its Jewish form, in which Mary gave birth to Jesus the Messiah, and then in its Christian form, in which it was persecuted by a political power as evil as the dragon (12:6). We should note the continuity here in John's mind.

In the next scene the dragon, apparently angered by his failure to kill the newborn Messiah, engages in war with Michael and his angels (12:7-9). The archangel Michael was regarded as the heavenly patron of Israel (Daniel 10:13, 21; 12:1), and so, by extension, of the new people of God. Michael defeats the dragon and casts him out of heaven down to earth. The dragon's defeat and eviction from heaven are the cause of great rejoicing by the remaining heavenly dwellers (Revelation 12:10-12). In Christ's victory, the victory of his people is included:

*"They have conquered him [the devil] by the blood of
the Lamb
    and by the word of their testimony,
for they did not cling to life even in the face of death.
Rejoice then, you heavens
    and those who dwell in them!"*

(12:11-12a)

The words of the triumph song remind us that the vision of Michael fighting the dragon is symbolic, representing the real victory won by the atoning death of Christ—a victory in which Christians participate by their unflinching witness to Christ and his kingdom. Martyrdom is portrayed once again as the path not to shameful defeat but to glorious conquest over God's enemies.

The last verses of the chapter show Satan's persistent hostility against the church and his persecution of the faithful. Obviously, John uses metaphorical language to communicate spiritual realities (the earth has no "mouth," verse 16). In furious wrath the dragon begins to inflict great harm on the woman's other children (12:17)—that is, on Christians who obey God and bear testimony to Jesus. By this retrospective tableau the author explains how the persecution of Christians began. He charges the devil with the primary responsibility for initiating it, but it represents the desperation and frustration of an already-defeated enemy.

In Revelation chapter 13, two of Satan's agents appear. These two, along with the dragon, comprise something like a counterfeit trinity.[1] One is a frightful beast, rising out of the sea, who is given power by the dragon. This beast with its many heads symbolizes the Roman Empire with its rulers, which John understood to be in competition with Christ for the allegiance and worship of "every tribe and people and language and nation" (13:7-8; compare 5:9-10). The beast, we are told, "opened its mouth to utter blasphemies against God" (13:6), reviling God's name and his heavenly dwelling. We know what this means. Beginning with Julius Caesar, Roman emperors had been deified, that is, were given the status and worship due to a god, the early ones after their deaths, but later emperors even during their lifetimes. Some emperors, like Domitian, appear to have taken an overt liking to this practice, insisting on being addressed as "lord and god." All of the cities to which John was writing had multiple temples, shrines, and open-air altars dedicated to these "deities"—a mockery of the heavenly dwelling of the one true God.

The cult of the emperors was generally promoted from below, and quite enthusiastically by the elites of the province of Asia Minor in particular. These local supporters of the worship of the beast are seen in the second beast, which rises up from the land (13:11). John would later call this second beast the "false prophet" (16:13), the preacher of the idolatrous cult that set itself against the worship of the Creator God. In this sense, it is a personification of paganism itself. With a grim parody John describes the beast as having "two horns like a lamb"—that is, it has taken on the guise of God's chosen one, yet "it spoke like a dragon" (13:11). This agent of the dragon promoted the worship of the emperor by means of all kinds of spectacular tricks of bogus religion (13:13-15), even causing the image of the first beast to appear to be alive. The priests of the traditional pagan gods were not strangers to using special effects to impress the worshipers.

One of the ways a ruler impressed his sovereignty most vividly on the minds of his subjects was by issuing coins bearing his image and title. Throughout the Roman Empire, every transaction of buying and selling, if it involved the transfer of money, meant handling imperial coins. Around the head of the emperor on a coin were titles, often including references to being the son of a deified predecessor and an object of reverence himself (the sense of *Augustus*, which became a title that all emperors bore). John may be thinking of such coins when he speaks of the mark of the beast, without which "no one can buy or sell" (13:17). Consequently, resistance by Christians to the cult of the emperor would entail the very worst consequences—being subject to economic problems as well as to persecution.

The details of John's vision are symbolic. Thus, the "mark" on the right hand or the forehead (13:16) is meant figuratively. Those who conform to the demands of the state are given means to identify themselves so that they can claim the benefits due to them.

The famous "number of the beast" is mentioned at the end of chapter 13. The number "six hundred sixty-six" is, in the first place, a symbol of the greatest imperfection, for it is the sacred number seven less one, repeated thrice. John says that it is a human number; that is, it is the number of a person's name. In Greek, Latin, and Hebrew, the letters of the alphabet also served as numerals, and it was a well-known technique to add up the letters that comprise a proper name and use the sum to identify the person in a kind of code. A graffito in a latrine in Pompeii reads, "I love her whose number is 545," inviting the next person to pass the time relieving himself to try to figure out which girl in Pompeii he had meant by adding up the letters in various candidate's names.

Who is this satanic beast, symbolized by the number 666? Over the centuries a very great deal of ingenuity has been expended in attempting to answer this question. A further complication arises from the fact that some ancient manuscripts of the Book of Revelation give the number as 616 instead of 666.

Among the names and titles that have been proposed to solve the cryptogram, the most probable candidate is the emperor Nero.

If we add the numerical values in the Hebrew[2] spelling of the name Neron Caesar, we obtain 666; on the other hand, since his name can equally well be spelled without the last N, if we omit the final N, the total will be 616. There does not appear to be any other name, or a name with a title, that satisfies *both* 666 and 616.

The profound religious insight that lies behind these kaleidoscopic pictures in chapter 13 is that men and women are so constituted as to worship some absolute power, and if they do not worship the true and real Power behind the universe, they will construct a god for themselves and give allegiance to that. In the last analysis, it is always a choice between the power that operates through domination and inflicting suffering (that is, the power of the beast) and the power that operates through redeeming and restoring, even at the cost of *accepting* suffering (that is, the power of the Lamb).

Following the account of the dragon's war against God and its most recent manifestation in the rise of the beast and its cult, John once again provides a second panel to create a diptych. His readers are presented with the alternatives of gathering around the image of the beast out of fear of the consequences (13:11-18) or standing bravely beside the Lamb assured of the better consequences that attend such allegiance (14:1-5).

The first part of Revelation chapter 14 is a scene of tranquility and rejoicing. John sees the Lamb, standing on Mount Zion, with the 144,000 of the redeemed. As was mentioned earlier (see p. 76), 144,000 is a symbolic number, representing all those who remain faithful in the midst of the challenges of life in John's world. Here he adds a puzzling detail: "It is these who have not defiled themselves with women, for they are virgins" (14:4). On the surface this suggests that only men who have never had sexual intercourse can "follow the Lamb wherever he goes." There are many reasons, however, to reject a literal understanding of this sentence. First, the rest of the Bible sanctions and commends marriage, and so one hesitates to understand this as a condemnation of marriage or a demand for celibacy. Second, John uses a great deal of sexual imagery throughout the book. In a world in which the great political power is a whore (14:8; 17:1-5), the holy community of God a bride (19:6-8; 21:9-10), and the preacher of a deviant gospel an adulteress (2:21-22), one suspects that a group of 144,000 "virgins" are to be understood figuratively. John, indeed, appears to adopt the imagery found frequently in the Old Testament where any contact with pagan worship was called "fornication" or "adultery." Hence, the 144,000 are those who have not defiled themselves by participating in the idolatrous cults that everywhere surround the converts to the worship of the one God. It is regrettable that John chose to perpetuate the use of imagery, however figurative, that casts women *tout court* in the role of that which defiles and disqualifies.

Once again the hearers of Revelation are confronted with options—options that a Jezebel or a Nicolaitan would argue are not mutually exclusive, but that John would set in stark opposition one to the other. Either one gives to God and the Lamb—and them alone—the worship and loyalty that are their due, or one finds oneself ranged alongside the minions of the dragon in their rebellion against God and the Lamb, with fearsome consequences.

9

THE SEVEN BOWLS OF GOD'S WRATH

(Revelation 14:6–16:21)

Revelation 14:6-20 is perhaps the clearest portion of the book. The messages of the three angels and the pronouncement of the Spirit are the "three points and the poem" that stand at the core of the strange sermon that John preaches (14:6-13). The visions of judgment that follow in 14:14-20 are as straightforward as Jesus' own parables about the gathering in of the elect and the elimination of the rebels.

John sees an "angel flying in midheaven, with an eternal gospel to proclaim to those who live on the earth" (14:6). The angel says in a loud voice, "Fear God and give him glory, for the hour of his judgment has come; and worship him who made heaven and earth, the sea and the springs of water" (14:7). Worship rightly directed is a major focus for John in his setting. The angel's pronouncement reminds John's hearers of two principal reasons to make the wise choice in regard to worship: as Creator and Sustainer of all that is, God alone merits worship and ultimate allegiance (see 4:11); and because God will hold all creation accountable to God's commandments, this is the only advantageous course of action in the long run!

Another angel announces the fall of Babylon (14:8), a theme that John will take up later in great detail (see 17:1–18:24). This simple pronouncement asserts the ultimate disadvantage of seeking partnership with Rome, whether through making room for the cultic rites that the Christians' neighbors demand of them or through profiting from Rome's exploitative economy. God has already determined that Rome is a fallen power; in God's sight trafficking with Rome is "fornication." What is truly to be gained by negotiating an alliance with the Roman system at the cost of clear allegiance to God?

A third angel announces eternal condemnation for those who persist in worshiping the beast and its image—who give to the dragon's bully and puppet the honor that is due the one God. Such people, he declares, will "drink the wine of God's wrath...and they will be tormented with fire and sulfur.... And the smoke of their torment goes up forever and ever. There is no rest day or night for those who worship the beast and its image" (14:10-11).

This passage gives offense to some modern readers of Revelation; certainly it sounds terribly vindictive and gruesome. But since elsewhere in the Book of Revelation the author uses metaphors and symbolic language, it would be quite unfair to take him literally here and to think of God roasting rebels for eternity in a lake of fiery, molten sulfur. Nevertheless, the language ought to communicate something about the seriousness of persistently rejecting God. Throughout Revelation we have seen that if people persist in living contrary to the structure of God's universe, they must suffer. John's words here mean that the most terrible thing that a person can do is deliberately to turn away from the living God. Such torment, says John, is "forever and ever." This is so, because God respects our free will and will never force us to turn to him. So this picture of wrath and hell means nothing more or less than the terrible truth that the sufferings of those who persist in rejecting God's love in Christ are self-imposed and self-perpetuated. The inevitable consequence is that if they persist in such rejection, God will never violate their personality. Whether any soul will in fact eternally resist God, we cannot say.

These solemn thoughts are followed by words of comfort, which comprise the second of the seven beatitudes contained in the Book of Revelation. John hears a voice from heaven declaring, "'Blessed are the dead who from now on die in the Lord.' 'Yes,' says the Spirit, 'they will rest from their labors, for their deeds follow them'" (14:13). Their good deeds and patient sufferings will follow them as witnesses for them before the Judge of the living and the dead (see pp. 124–125).

Suddenly John takes us once again to the Last Day (14:14-20). We see a more extended vision of "the Son of Man coming on the clouds of heaven" to gather his elect (Matthew 24:30-31). What John shows us, however, is a double vision. "One like the Son of Man" puts in his sickle to reap "the harvest of the earth" (14:14-16). Every indication suggests that this act is a good thing. The 144,000 were the "first fruits for God and the Lamb" (14:4); now the whole harvest of God's faithful ones are gathered in. The second episode, however, is unambiguously negative. Isaiah's vision of the judgment of Edom (Isaiah 63:1-6) is the prototype for a final, universal treading of "the great wine press of the wrath of God" (14:19). The veritable sea of blood that results speaks of John's expectations of the vast number of human beings who will have ended their lives still estranged from, even enemies of, the one God.

In Revelation chapters 15 through 18 the judgments of God and the struggle of the church in its conflict with hostile world powers reach new levels of intensity. Earlier in Revelation chapter 6 we were told of the opening of the seven seals (see pp. 69–78), followed in chapters 8 and 9 by the seven trumpets announcing additional woes (see pp. 79–84). Now in Revelation chapters 15 and 16 we come to an account of the seven bowls full of God's wrath poured successively by each of the seven angels on the earth, on the sea, on the rivers and fountains, on the sun, on the throne of the beast, on the great River Euphrates, and finally into the air (16:2-17). These are described as "seven plagues, which are the last, for with them the wrath of God is ended" (15:1). While the trumpets announced judgments that affected only a fraction of the earth, the devastation of the bowls (many of which specifically recall the judgments of the trumpets) is now total. There is indeed "no more delay" (10:6), no more leaving room for repentance. The orderliness and relentlessness of these unfolding series—the seals, the trumpets, the bowls—itself communicates something about God's control over history and the measured inexorability of the end that God has decreed for it.

Prior to the opening of the seventh seal (8:1-2), which introduced the seven trumpet woes, John portrayed the security of God's faithful by telling of the 144,000 that had been sealed and the great multitude in white robes (see pp. 75–78). Now, before describing the seven plagues of divine wrath, John portrays the safety of "those who had conquered the beast and its image and the number of its name" (15:2). These victors, with harps of God in their hands, "sing the song of Moses . . . and the song of the Lamb" (15:3). In Exodus 15:1-18, the words of the song of Moses after crossing the Red Sea are very different from those of the song of the Lamb. John is not suggesting that they were the same song. But it is appropriate to recall the Song of Moses celebrating the Exodus from Egypt here on the shore of another sea, celebrating God's greater, universal Exodus. The song of the redeemed in Revelation 15:3-4, moreover, echoes a major theme of Moses' Song: "Who is like you, O LORD, among the gods . . . awesome in splendor, doing wonders?" (Exodus 15:11).

The song expresses confidence that all nations will be led to worship the one true God, because they will acknowledge the justice of what he has done in vindicating his people. As the seer listens to the song, it swells into an anthem that celebrates the mercies of the Lord God. The song consists almost entirely of phrases taken verbatim from various parts of the Old Testament (compare Psalm 111:2; 139:14; Deuteronomy 32:4; Psalm 145:17; Jeremiah 10:7; Psalm 96:9). John expresses here his conviction that the "old songs" celebrating God's character and God's inevitable interventions in the human sphere will yet prove true in God's future—and thus provide reliable bases for hope in the present. The structure of the song reflects the parallelism characteristic of the Hebrew poetry upon which it draws.

> *"Great and amazing are your deeds,*
> *Lord God the Almighty!*
> *Just and true are your ways,*
> *King of the nations!*
> *Lord, who will not fear*
> *and glorify your name?*

> *For you alone are holy.*
> *All nations will come*
> *and worship before you,*
> *for your judgments have been revealed."*

(15:3-4)

One of the most striking features of this song of the triumphant martyrs is the absence of any mention of their own victory and their own achievement. From beginning to end the whole song is a lyrical outburst celebrating the greatness of God. The hymn itself, like other songs in Revelation, may have been used in the early church. They make some of our modern ephemeral ditties appear incredibly trite.

Following the victors' song of praise, John sees that "the temple of the tent of witness in heaven was opened" (15:5), and out of it came seven angels, "robed in pure bright linen, with golden sashes across their chests. Then one of the four living creatures gave the seven angels seven golden bowls full of the wrath of God" (15:6-7). The Greek word for "bowls" denotes vessels that are broad and shallow, shaped like a saucer, so that their contents can be poured out completely and suddenly. They ironically resemble the very bowls used by Greek and Roman priests to pour out offerings over the fires on the altars of their rival gods. John adds the ominous detail that access to God in God's heavenly sanctuary is now blocked until the bowls of judgment are poured out (15:8). There will be no interceding, no relenting, at this late stage.

John then hears a loud voice from the temple telling the seven angels, "Go and pour out on the earth the seven bowls of the wrath of God" (16:1). This destruction is directed against those "who had the mark of the beast and who worshiped its image" (16:2). Thereupon the bowls of God's wrath are emptied. This succession of plagues is not to be understood as an orgy of indiscriminate destruction, but as the working out of God's justice in judgment upon those who worship the beast and have upheld its reign and its ills. The repeated emphasis on their lack of repentance indicates their true allegiance insofar as they blaspheme the living God (16:9, 11).

The author's descriptive details of the plagues contribute to the general effect of intense calamity and terror. The unmistakable reminiscences once again of the plagues of Exodus—blood, darkness, sores, frogs, hail—communicate John's conviction that the just God who judged Egypt for its oppression of God's people must inevitably act again, and decisively, against the oppressive and self-serving domination systems of the world that violate the moral structure of God's universe. Like a good teacher, John repeats with kaleidoscopic variety his central conviction that God rules and overrules in the affairs of the church and the world. We might say that John sets up several mirrors in which the same objects are reflected from different sides, so that the reader cannot fail to take note of them.

At the same time, there is an unmistakable progression. The seventh in each of the first two series of judgments produces another series, similar to the previous series but more terrible. Following the opening of the seals, the second series of trumpets ushers in new disasters, which are blasts of warning, calling men and women to repentance. By the time of the third series, the summons to repentance having proved to be unheeded, further judgments are poured out from the bowls of God's wrath—a picture of swift, uninterrupted, and complete punishment.

John's motive for describing such a prolonged sequence appears to have been a desire to prepare the church for a period of suffering, even as he assures his congregations that their oppressors stand under God's dreadful judgment. Although he is confident that the Lord will come soon and bring deliverance, he does not want to delude his readers with hopes that may be premature. Nothing in the book is more remarkable than the grim honesty with which the writer faces the situation before him. Of course he desires to comfort his fellow-sufferers, but he does not comfort them with any false hopes. Fully conscious of the calamities that await it, the church must prepare to meet them undaunted.

This sequence brings us at last to what is commonly called the battle of Armageddon. When the sixth angel has emptied his bowl of doom, a strange and unusual happening takes place (16:13). Foul spirits like frogs come from the mouth of the dragon, the mouth of the first beast, and the mouth of the second beast, identified here as the false prophet. These foul spirits, pictured as demonic frogs more dreadful than those of the Egyptian plague of frogs in the time of Moses (Exodus 8:2-14), perform signs in an attempt to deceive the kings of the earth. The frogs and their croaking represent generally the ability to deceive by means of superstitions, preposterous claims, and lies. Propaganda, unscrupulously used by totalitarian states, would certainly be a modern illustration of this picture. John sees these demonic spirits as going abroad in order to assemble the kings of the whole world for a battle that is to occur at a place called Armageddon (Revelation 16:16).

This mouth-filling word, like the number 666, has been magnified in popular thinking out of all proportion to its significance as a word. Curiously enough, no one knows for certain what the name *Armageddon* means. First, we do not really know how to spell it. In some Greek manuscripts of Revelation, it is spelled Harmagedon. The scribes of other manuscripts spell the word with one *d* and two *g*'s; others with two *d*'s and one *g*; others still with two *g*'s and two *d*'s. In spite of the difficulty of knowing how to spell the word, and consequently what it means and where the place is located, most scholars suppose that it alludes to the mountain of Megiddo. The difficulty with this, however, is that there is no "Mount Megiddo"; Megiddo was the name of a city that gave its name to the pass between the coastal plains of Palestine and the Plain of Esdraelon. Because this had been the scene of frequent and decisive battles in ancient times (Judges 5:19-21; 2 Kings 9:27; 23:29), it would appear that John is using familiar language to symbolize the final great conflict between the forces of good and the forces of evil, a battle in which evil will be defeated—not by armaments but by God's incarnate Word, Jesus Christ (Revelation 19:13).

Finally, the seventh angel pours out his bowl (16:17). The impact of this plague is even greater as there is no interlude here between the sixth and seventh bowls as there had been between the sixth and seventh seals and between the sixth and seventh trumpets. A mighty voice out of the heavenly temple cries, "It is done!" Judgment day for Babylon has arrived (16:19). Amid natural catastrophes of unprecedented ferocity, Babylon falls. The seven plagues end with a bombardment of massive hailstones, each weighing about a hundred pounds (16:21). The fall of "Babylon" becomes the focal point of the lengthy section to follow (17:1–18:24), as John catalogs the crimes of Roman domination and anticipates God's inevitable judgments.

10

BABYLON THE GREAT: TOPPLING EMPIRE AND ITS EVILS

(Revelation 17:1–18:24)

Revelation chapters 17 and 18 are a literary triumph of imaginative power. More than once John had found comfort for himself and his people by proclaiming the fall of Rome. So certain is he that God will judge the persecutors of the church that he now devotes two chapters to an account of the crashing down of the fabulous "grandeur that was Rome." To say directly that God will destroy imperial Rome would have been, of course, altogether treasonous in the eyes of the imperial authorities. So, like a prisoner writing in code from a concentration camp, John characterizes the power of evil as Babylon (though a Roman official of even moderate intelligence could not fail to see his mother city reflected in a text that spoke of a city set on seven hills that held dominion over the kings of the earth [17:9, 18]). Just as Babylon represented to the Hebrews all that was wicked and symbolized persecution, so for John, Rome was another Babylon, the source and fountainhead of all seductive luxury and vice, living in voluptuous materialism and selfishness.

This is not merely an expedient to avoid trouble. John knows and harnesses the power of historical precedent. He and his hearers know Scripture's diagnosis and condemnation of earlier seats of empire like Babylon and their practices (see Ezekiel 27–28; Isaiah 23; Jeremiah 51). They know the fate of the Babylonian empire. By presenting Rome in the guise of Babylon and reconfiguring the ancient prophets' denunciations, John intensifies and grounds his hearers' expectations for the fate of the new iteration of Babylon, the new seat of empire that has set itself up quite blatantly against God, God's vision for human community, and God's faithful worshipers.

John paints a startling picture of Rome. The inhabitants of each of the seven cities housing the Christians John addresses could walk past, or see on the change in their pockets, representations of Rome as a goddess. This was the ultimate legitimation of Rome's power and authority, that she should be proclaimed—and dutifully worshiped by her subjects!—as a divinity in her own right. She might appear robed in a stately dress, the female counterpart to the toga; more often she appeared in her military garb, a reminder of Rome's victory in conquest and in the suppression of revolts against her rule. John shows her here in her evening wear—in her true colors and her unmasked persona. She is not the instrument by which the gods would bring peace, order, and rule of law to the whole world, as Virgil claimed in his brilliant piece of propaganda, the *Aeneid*. She is an instrument of defilement, spreading her filth and involving people in her crimes across the entire Mediterranean.

Look at her, says John. Dressed in purple and scarlet, she is resplendent and seductive, "adorned with gold and jewels and pearls" (17:4). Instead of having a scepter in her hand, she is holding a golden cup that is filled with the impurities of her fornications, the abominations of her idolatries. Seated on a scarlet beast that is covered with blasphemous names (the collective emperors that we met in 13:1-10), the woman personifies imperial power and oppression. The statement that "the kings of the earth have committed fornication" with her (17:2) must be understood metaphorically to mean that Rome has usurped and perverted the political power of all her provinces, enticing or forcing originally independent people groups to live under her yoke.

She is drunk, not with wine, but with the lifeblood of the witnesses of Jesus whom she caused to be slain (17:6). The reference here is to wild orgies of persecution, such as those instigated by Nero and described by the Roman historian Tacitus. According to that non-Christian writer, in the 60s of the first century, "a vast multitude of Christians were not only put to death, but put to death with insult. They were either clothed in the skins of wild beasts and then exposed in the arena to the attacks of half-famished dogs, or else dipped in tar and put on crosses to be set on fire, and, when the daylight failed, to be burned as lights by night" (*Annals* 15.44). Tacitus comments that Nero's persecution of Christians was so terrible that even non-Christian citizens were horrified and began to intercede in their behalf.

In Revelation chapter 18, John describes the fall of Rome with pathos and realism. The literature of the world contains few passages that compare in dramatic power with this dirge over the fallen city. Like the tolling of a funeral bell, we hear the repeated lamentation: "Alas, alas, the great city!" (18:10, 16, 19). Despite all her sins and crimes, there are many who partnered with and profited from Roman imperialism, and who now mourn for her. The kings of the earth who had consorted with her "weep and wail over her when they see the smoke of her burning" (18:9). The merchants who became wealthy because of her great commerce and trade "weep and mourn for her, since no one buys their cargo anymore" (18:11).

If John had spent any time at all in Ephesus, he would indeed have seen massive amounts of the cargoes he lists moving toward the docks at the seaport to be loaded onto ships heading west toward Italy. Of course Rome's buyers could snatch up all the luxury goods offered on the market—cinnamon from far-off Sri Lanka (ancient Taprobane), ivory from Africa, pearls from India, marble from Asia Minor, Greece, and North Africa. But massive amounts of staples were also shipped off to Rome, such as grain to supply the bread that was distributed gratis to about two hundred thousand families, a perk of living in the capital city of a world empire! And Rome would get its grain in the set amounts at the set prices, no matter what that meant for access to grain in the provinces.

As the climax of this empire-wide cargo manifest of luxuries and necessities, John names "slaves—and human lives" (18:13). The essential inhumanity of Rome's exploitation of the empire clearly reveals itself by the constant flow of slaves from the provinces to the city of Rome. By John's time, slaves made up almost a third of the population of the city and a quarter of the population of the empire as a whole. Slave labor was the bedrock upon which the Roman economy was founded. The prosperity of the whole was tainted by the evil at its roots.

The NRSV renders the close of 18:13 as "slaves—and human lives," as if to name two separate items. A closer translation of these words would be "bodies, even human lives." John uses the demeaning but common word to refer to slaves—they were just "bodies" or, in Aristotle's infamous definition, "animate tools" (*Politics* 1.4). John rejects the dominant discourse about slaves and indicts the Roman slave trade. These are indeed "human lives" that are being traded on the market and subjugated entirely to the interests of the Roman economy. Perhaps the most egregious violation of human rights in this system is to be seen in the fate of those slaves who were slated to fight for their lives and to die for the entertainment of the Roman crowds in the amphitheaters built for that purpose by the Caesars. These victims, too, were among the delicious fruits to which Roman taste had become accustomed (18:14).

The shipmasters and sailors stand far off as the city burns and throw dust on their heads, crying out, "What city was like the great city?" ... "For in one hour she has been laid waste" (18:17-19). Here once again (as earlier in 18:9, 15), John allows us to see the fall of Rome from the perspective of those who had grown powerful and rich through their involvement with the city and its economic system. For such people, of course, Rome's downfall is also their own—no wonder they mourn! But from John's perspective, the fall of Rome is cause for rejoicing and praise of God (18:20; 19:1).

The chapter concludes with a remarkable passage (18:21-24) that describes with haunting power the tragic end of the city. In contrast to her former festivity, the daily activity of her busy artisans, and her domestic labors and joys, now all is silence and desolation and ruin. The dirge concludes (18:24) with the explanation that Rome is to be destroyed because of the blood of prophets and saints whom she has caused to be slaughtered—martyred, it is implied, because they had refused to take part in the cult of the emperor-gods.

John indicts Rome essentially on three charges: (1) it has perpetrated violence upon the peoples of the earth and against any who resisted or, like the Christians, bore witness to a different hope; (2) it has exploited its provinces for its own economic advantage and enjoyment of the lion's share of the world's produce; (3) it has exercised idolatrous arrogance in its claims on its own behalf, that it ruled by the will of the gods and would hold sway forever. It is no wonder, then, that the primary summons given to John's congregations would be: "Come out of her, my people, so that you do not take part in her sins, and so that you do not share in her plagues" (18:4). John knew centuries before modern critique of imperialism that one could not enjoy the profits of an unjust system without also sharing in the guilt of that unjust system, and he would have his congregations avoid the consequences of the latter. He therefore challenges Christian partnership with such a system in *any* way—economic, ideological, whatever—and calls instead for witness through withdrawal and nonparticipation, through refusing to accept Rome's propaganda. It is remarkable that when John wrote these immensely moving chapters about the fall of Rome, Rome was still enjoying undisputed sovereignty and undimmed prestige. So great, however, is John's faith in the sovereignty of God and his confidence that the justice of God must eventually punish evil that he writes as though Rome had already fallen. As with so many judgments of God, the fulfillment actually came slowly, but at last suddenly. For centuries Rome decayed and degenerated, moral poison infecting her whole life. Then during a fateful week in August of the year AD 410, Alaric, with his northern hordes of Goths, pillaged Rome and laid it waste.

What do we learn from this part of the Book of Revelation?

Certainly John wrote in order to stimulate faithfulness on the part of Christians persecuted by Rome and their neighbors, and to awaken Christians duped into seeking an easier compromise with the Roman machine. He assures them of the ultimate victory of Christ. But Revelation also has a warning for believers down through the years. John's indictment of Rome remains a warning to any nation that elevates material abundance, military prowess, technological sophistication, imperial grandeur, racial pride, and any other form of idolatry, the glorification of the creature over the Creator. It continues to admonish any human domination system that resists *God's* desires and vision for human community bound together by reverence for God and commitment to God's ideals for our treatment of one another and to call God's people to "come out" and stand apart from all practices that perpetuate such resistance (18:4). The challenge of Revelation 17 and 18 is not to try to identify what country or world power is this "Babylon" of prophecy; rather, it is to discern what is Babylonish in our own country and to learn how to disentangle ourselves from every practice that interferes with, or stands opposed to, the achievement of God's good desires for all people.

In these chapters we have an up-to-date portrait of what may occur when we idolize the gross national product, worship growth, and become so preoccupied with quantity that we ignore both quality and equality. The message of the Book of Revelation concerns the character and timeliness of God's judgment not only of persons but also of nations and, in fact, of all principalities and powers—which is to say, all authorities, corporations, institutions, structures, bureaucracies, and the like. And, to the extent that ecclesiastical denominations and sects have succumbed to the lure of power and prestige, the words of John are applicable also to present-day church structures.

11

THE FINAL VICTORY AND THE LAST JUDGMENT

(Revelation 19:1–20:15)

In contrast to the lament and dirges over the fall of Babylon in the previous chapter, the setting is now changed to heaven, where the voices of a great multitude are heard singing choruses that begin with "Hallelujah!"[1] (19:1-3). After celebrating the destruction of the profligate city, Babylon, the larger and more important part of the songs of praise looks to the future, the perfected union of Christ and his bride, the church. In this grand oratorio all the choirs of heaven unite. First, the twenty-four elders and the four living creatures fall down and worship "God who is seated on the throne, saying, 'Amen. Hallelujah!'" (19:4). Then a voice comes from the throne saying, "Praise our God, all you his servants, and all who fear him, small and great" (19:5). This comprehensive phrase, "small and great," includes believers of all classes and abilities, and of all stages of progress in their Christian life.

Finally, John hears "what seemed to be the voice of a great multitude, like the sound of many waters and like the sound of mighty thunderpeals" (19:6). The heavenly voices triumphantly announce:

> *"The Lord our God*
> > *the Almighty reigns.*
> *Let us rejoice and exult*
> > *and give him the glory,*
> *for the marriage of the Lamb has come,*
> > *and his bride has made herself ready."*
> > > *(19:6-7)*

The concept of the relationship between God and his people as a marriage goes far back into the Old Testament. Again and again the prophets spoke of Israel as the chosen bride of God (Isaiah 54:1-8; Ezekiel 16:7; Hosea 2:19). In the New Testament the church is represented as the bride of Christ; he loved the church so much that he gave himself up in her behalf (Ephesians 5:25). In the words of a familiar hymn: "With his own blood he bought her, and for her life he died."

As the majestic chorus of praise to God reaches its end, John hears a voice commanding him to record the fourth of the seven beatitudes found in the Book of Revelation: "Write this: Blessed are those who are invited to the marriage supper of the Lamb" (19:9). Mention of the wedding feast of Christ and his bride, the church, is a signal that the climax of the drama is very close at hand. Satan is about to be overthrown, and his dominion is nearing its end. From here on the tempo of the action increases. The ultimate outcome cannot be in doubt, but there are some surprises ahead, with the suspense of the drama sustained to the conclusion.

From verse 11 in chapter 19 to the end of chapter 20, we have in rapid succession seven visions preparatory to the end. Each of these begins with the words "I saw" (19:11, 17, 19; 20:1, 4, 11, 12). Out of the opened heaven there comes into John's view a white horse, symbolic of victory. Its rider is called "Faithful and True." He has piercing eyes like a flame of fire (as in 1:14), and on his head are many crowns ("diadems," crowns of royalty). The dragon and the beast had both worn multiple diadems as Satan exercised dominion over the kingdoms of the world through his agent (12:3; 13:1), but they must inevitably cede their power and dominion to God's Anointed: "The kingdom of the world has become the kingdom of our Lord and of his Messiah, and he will reign forever and ever" (11:15).

The rider, who is the conquering Christ, "is clothed in a robe dipped in blood" (19:13). This description recalls Isaiah 63:1-3, where the conqueror's garments are stained crimson with the blood of his Edomite enemies. But here John reshapes the imagery to portray the gospel of Christ who triumphed by shedding his own blood (see 5:6, 9). He is called "The Word of God" (19:13; compare John 1:1, 14). Christ's proper name is not meant here, but rather his office; it is through him that God has spoken fully and finally to us (see Hebrews 1:1-2). Following Christ are "the armies of heaven…on white horses"; instead of wearing armor, they are clad in "fine linen, white and pure" (19:14). As in the initial vision of the heavenly Christ (1:16), so too here "from his mouth comes a sharp sword with which to strike down the nations" (19:15). That sword is his word; it is his only armament. By it he convicts, exonerates, and executes judgment.

John sees "an angel standing in the sun" (19:17) who calls the vultures of the sky to gather at a great feast where they may gorge themselves on the corpses of those who have fallen in battle. The revolting scene is based on the visions of Ezekiel (chapters 38 and 39, especially 39:17-20) when God commands birds of every kind to gather for a feast on the warriors and princes of Gog. John freely adapts Ezekiel's account to his own use both here and in 20:7-10. This carrion meal is a solemn travesty of the marriage supper of the Lamb, an announcement of which has introduced this scene of punishment (19:9).

These statements are symbolic, not literal. Never shall we see the "white horse," or the sword projecting from the mouth of the conqueror, or the birds gorged with the flesh of fallen warriors (19:21). The descriptions are not descriptions of real occurrences, but of symbols of the real occurrences. The message that John conveys through this symbolism is that evil will surely be overthrown. Here that message is presented in apocalyptic pictures of almost repellent realism.

Now the final, great conflict between good and evil takes place. "The beast and the kings of the earth with their armies" (19:19) come face to face with Christ and his followers. This immensely critical moment has been in John's view from the beginning, and we might have expected to read details of how the battle went, with its different phases and critical moments. But the man of Patmos makes no statement about the battle, which is evidence that he intends to describe not an earthly military campaign but a spiritual struggle. He portrays only the result—the overwhelming defeat of the enemies of Christ. The beast is captured along with his chief lieutenant, the false prophet, who has been identified as the Roman religious cult (13:11-18). In the figurative language of apocalyptic, both are "thrown alive into the lake of fire that burns with sulfur" (19:20).

It is noteworthy that the victory is won by Christ's word alone without any military help from the faithful. This picture contrasts sharply with other apocalypses of the period and, in particular, with the War Scroll of the Qumran sect. According to these documents the military help of the faithful is necessary; in fact, the Qumran scroll gives precise directives for the disposition and weapons of the front formations and for the disposition and movements of the cavalry (War Scroll, cols. 5-6).

Having related the destruction of the beast and the false prophet, John now turns to the ultimate enemy who deceived the nations, identified by four sinister names: the dragon, the ancient serpent, the devil, or Satan. John sees an angel descend from heaven with a chain in his hand and with the key to the bottomless pit (20:1). The angel seizes Satan, binds him with the chain, and locks him in the pit for a thousand years (20:3).

During this period the souls of those who had died a martyr's death because they would not worship the beast come to life and reign with Christ for a thousand years. Whether it is these or another group not otherwise identified that are "given authority to judge" (20:4), John does not say. Nor does he say that Christ and those who come to life return to the earth for these thousand years. In any case, however, John carefully distinguishes the martyrs from all others, going so far as to say that none of the rest of the dead come to life in this millennial blessedness (20:5). Their resurrection appears to be spiritual and not corporeal. A beatitude (the fifth of the seven in Revelation) is pronounced on those who participate in this resurrection (20:6). "The second death has no power" over them and as "priests of God and of Christ" they will enjoy unimaginable exaltation, security, and blessedness. Their patient endurance of persecution was, by comparison, for only a short time.

After the thousand years Satan is released for a little while (20:3, 7). Just why this is done, and by whom, is an undisclosed mystery. Now Satan resumes his deception of the nations, and instigates two mysterious figures, Gog and Magog, as his obedient tools (20:8). The prophet Ezekiel refers to "Gog, of the land of Magog, the chief prince of Meshech and Tubal" (Ezekiel 38:2), who will come from the north against God's people living peacefully in the land. The limited scope of Ezekiel's oracles is expanded in Revelation to cosmic proportions. Whereas in Ezekiel Magog is the territory of which Gog is the ruler, here (as well as in Jewish rabbinic literature) Gog and Magog are parallel names, used together of the world powers opposed to God. It is altogether misguided ingenuity to attempt to identify specific nations today as Gog and Magog, for John says these nations are innumerable (Revelation 20:8).

With their armies they besiege "the beloved city" (this would be Jerusalem if a literal city is intended). The situation appears to be desperate, but fire quite opportunely comes down from heaven and consumes Gog and Magog and their armies (20:9). Following their defeat, Satan is captured once more, and this time he is thrown into the lake of fire and sulfur, whither his cohorts, the beast and the false prophet, had been consigned (see 19:20). Here the unholy trio "will be tormented day and night forever" (20:10). Satan's rule is now completely and absolutely finished, and his world-age is ended forever.

Such is the account of the thousand-year period in chapter 20 of Revelation—the only place in the Bible that mentions the millennium. The word *millennium* is a Latin term that means one thousand years. Over the centuries, diverse interpretations have been built on these few verses. Commentators have read into John's account ideas from other parts of the Bible (such as the rapture, the tribulation, the reconstruction of the Jewish temple), none of which are mentioned here. Such elaborations generally fall into one of three principal schools of interpretation.

1. Postmillennialists believe that Christ will come after the millennium has taken place. The kingdom of God is now being extended in the world through the preaching of the gospel and the saving work of the Holy Spirit. Christ is already reigning through his obedient church and will bring to the world a thousand years of peace and righteousness prior to his return at the conclusion of history.

2. Premillennialists maintain that Christ will come before the millennium begins. Despite all attempts to Christianize society, things will become worse and worse, and in the last days Antichrist will gain control of human affairs. Only the catastrophic return of Christ can inaugurate the golden age of one thousand years of peace here on earth.

3. Amillennialists regard the thousand years, like other numerals in Revelation, to be symbolic. Instead of being a literal period of exactly one thousand years, the expression refers to a very long time, extending from the first coming of Christ to his Second Coming. During this entire period Satan's power is limited by the preaching of the gospel (Luke 10:18). The "last days" began with Jesus (Hebrews 1:2) and with the outpouring of the Holy Spirit on the day of Pentecost (Acts 2:16, 17), and they will end when the "last day" arrives (John 6:39, 40, 44, 54; 11:24; 12:48). Instead of the optimism of the postmillenarian or the pessimism of the premillenarian, the amillenarian takes seriously the realism of Jesus' parable of the weeds among the wheat (Matthew 13:24-30, 36-43), namely,

that good and evil will develop side by side until the harvest, which is at the end of the world.

Each of these interpretations involves various difficulties,[2] but the central truth of all three is the clear and direct affirmation: Christ will return, as he had promised (John 14:3), and will destroy the forces of evil and establish God's eternal kingdom.

John's next vision is one of awesome and sobering impressiveness; it is a vision of the Last Judgment (20:11-15). He sees a great white throne—it is great because it is God's throne, and it is white because of God's eternal purity. Next a most astounding thing occurs: the earth and the heaven, John says, "fled from [God's] presence, and no place was found for them" (20:11). That is, the one seated on the throne is so radiant and consuming that earth and sky vanish like dew in the sun. Then all the dead, without respect of persons, are brought before the judgment seat of God. The "great and small," that is, those who were important and those who were unimportant in this life, are assembled together; there are no absentees and there are no exemptions. Next John tells us that books are opened. One book can be called the book of merit, for it contains a record and remembrance of all the deeds of each one who stands before the throne of God. The notion that what we do—or fail to do—with our lives in the body matters eternally pervades the thinking of Jesus and his apostles (see Matthew 7:21-23; 25:31-46; Romans 2:6-11; 2 Corinthians 5:9-10; Galatians 6:7-10). Our theologies of salvation cannot ignore these passages in favor of others. Another book is the book of life, which belongs to the Lamb (Revelation 13:8; 21:27); this can be called the book of mercy. Here the work of Christ, who died to ransom his people and save them from their sin, is put on the credit side of the ledger, along with the names of all who are destined for acquittal and blessedness. It is a book from which, however, names can also be stricken where not accompanied by the fruits of loyalty to the Redeemer (3:5).

That books will be consulted in the Final Judgment is an idea found in many ancient traditions. Besides nonbiblical sources,[3] the conception of a heavenly register of the elect is mentioned in various parts of the Old Testament (for example, Exodus 32:32-33; Psalm 69:28; Daniel 7:10; Malachi 3:16). While we cannot conceive of actual books being written to record our lives, there is a sense in which the term *books* carries a deep and significant meaning. John obviously found the symbolism of the book of life to be suggestive, for he refers to it five times throughout Revelation (3:5; 13:8; 17:8; 20:12-15; and 21:27).[4]

The giving up of the dead by "the sea" and by "Death and Hades" signifies that all the dead are raised and brought to judgment. The manner and the place of dying make no difference; all are judged "according to what they had done" (20:13)—for there is no other way that impartial judgment can be rendered (see 1 Corinthians 3:11-15). Finally the two great enemies of humankind—Death and Hades, which are here personified—are destroyed after giving up the dead that were in them (Revelation 20:13). These voracious monsters that devour mortals are now overcome and have no more power over humankind (compare 6:8). They are thrown into the lake of fire, appropriately called "the second death" (20:14). The first death (which is but the shadow of death) is of the body alone; the "second death," which is absolute unmitigated death, is final and complete separation from God, the source of life (see Matthew 10:28; Luke 12:4-5). The last verse of the chapter contains the most poignant statement of all: "Anyone whose name was not found written in the book of life was thrown into the lake of fire" (Revelation 20:15).

The account in these few verses, in spite of their brevity, is one of the most impressive descriptions of the Last Judgment ever written. John's vision presents these truths better than any reasoned argument could ever do. The opening of the books suggests that our earthly lives are important and meaningful, and are taken into account at the end. But the consultation of the book of life shows that our eternal destiny is determined by God's decision, by God's grace, by God's amazing goodness.

The Final Judgment clears the scene for the establishment of the new heaven and the new earth, from which sin and imperfection and death are banished forevermore—as John's vision that follows reveals.

12

JOHN'S VISION OF THE HEAVENLY JERUSALEM

(Revelation 21:1–22:21)

Chapters 21 and 22 provide a magnificent climax for the last book of the Bible. In the opening verses of chapter 21, John gives a short, general description of the holy city, the new Jerusalem, which he will fill out in the succeeding verses. First there is a description of the eternal blessedness of God's people in the new heaven and the new earth. Here John elaborates on the promise God had long before given to Isaiah that he would "create new heavens and a new earth" (Isaiah 65:17), which would abide forever (Isaiah 66:22).

Whether John would have us think of the new heavens and new earth as a transformation of the existing order, or whether this present cosmos will come to an end and a new creation will replace it, is not quite clear. In any case, the word *new* used by John does not mean simply another, but a new kind of heaven and earth. The new creation will have some continuity with creation as we now know it, yet it will be radically different. What makes it new is disclosed in the opening paragraph. Here John lays the fullest emphasis upon that without which any heaven would be but the shadow of a name—he emphasizes the presence of God. In the new order God's home will be with God's people.

> *"He will dwell with them;*
> *they will be his peoples,*
> *and God himself will be with them;*
> *he will wipe every tear from their eyes.*
> *Death will be no more;*
> *mourning and crying and pain will be no more,*
> *for the first things have passed away."*
>
> *(21:3-4)*

Likewise in the new order, John tells us, there is to be no more sea (21:1). Behind this strange announcement lies the fact that the Jews regarded the sea as a symbol of separation and turbulence. Throughout the Bible it symbolizes restless insubordination (see Job 38:8-11; Psalm 89:9; Isaiah 57:20), and in Revelation 13:1 it casts up the system that embodies hostility against God's people. Naturally, then, there is no room for it in the new creation.

The positive side of that blessedness "when the sea is no more" is pictured by a description of "the holy city, the new Jerusalem, coming down out of heaven from God, prepared as a bride adorned for her husband" (21:2). That is to say, the city originates in heaven and is beautiful beyond all comparison. The heavenly Jerusalem, John is told later (21:9-10), represents the church, and a description of that city is given in the closing vision of the book (21:9–22:5).

And now, for only the second time in the book (1:8), God speaks. Seated on the throne God declares, "See, I am making all things new" (21:5). Although these words refer primarily to the final renewing at the end, the present tense also suggests that God is continually making things new here and now (compare 2 Corinthians 3:18; 4:16-18; 5:16-17; Colossians 3:1-4). Again, the mighty voice of God is heard saying, "It is done!" (21:6). To the mind of the believer the consummation of all that had been predicted and promised is so certain that in a sense it may be said to have been reached before it is actually accomplished. At every stage of the struggle the believer is conscious of the final victory. Very appropriately the divine name is mentioned to underscore the completion of everything that God began: "I am the Alpha and the Omega, the beginning and the end" (21:6).

To all who are thirsty God promises to "give water as a gift from the spring of the water of life" (21:6). In lands where water is such an essential commodity, salvation is beautifully described by the symbolism of a spring and a river (22:1). The free offer of the gospel sounds clearly and repeatedly in these last two chapters.

At this point John expands his initial announcement concerning the new Jerusalem and presents an elaborate description of the heavenly city (21:9–22:5). He tells us that one of the seven angels who had the bowls of wrath spoke to him saying, "Come, I will show you the bride, the wife of the Lamb" (21:9). The angel is no doubt the one who in chapter 17 summoned John to witness the judgment of the great whore (the wicked city of Babylon). At that time John was carried away in spirit into a wilderness; now, by contrast, he is carried away in spirit to a great, high mountain so as to get, as it were, a better vision of "the holy city Jerusalem coming down out of heaven from God" (21:10).

The fact that John refers twice (21:2, 10; see also 3:12) to the holy city as "coming down" does not mean that he saw the city come down from heaven on two separate occasions. John is identifying a permanent characteristic of the city; its nature is defined by its having come down. The expression involves more than a spatial metaphor: the city comes from God—it is not merely a voluntary association of men and women. With a sovereign disregard of rules against mixing metaphors, the beloved community (the church) is portrayed as both bride (21:9) and city (21:10-14), offering a clear alternative to Rome, portrayed as both prostitute (17:1-18) and city (17:18–18:24), and its systems of domination. In the following description of the New Jerusalem and its magnificence, therefore, the author presents at the same time a vision of heaven in a tapestry of symbolism that describes the church triumphant in its perfected and eternal glory.

Although John's description of the city (the people of God) is meant to be symbolic, it is nevertheless pictured very precisely. The angel who was talking to John "had a measuring rod of gold to measure the city and its gates and walls" (21:15). The city measures fifteen hundred miles in length, in breadth, and in height (21:16). But how can a city be a cube? The description is architecturally preposterous if taken literally, but communicates a profound spiritual hope. The New Jerusalem has dimensions that echo the Holy of Holies in the desert tabernacle and in the Jerusalem Temple, both of which were cubes. The quality of access to and face-to-face communion with God represented by the Holy of Holies will be open to all who are included in the New Jerusalem—who have lived as faithful citizens of the kingdom of God in the midst of the regime of Babylon. It is the visual depiction of the affirmation celebrated just a few paragraphs before: "See, the home of God is among mortals. He will dwell with them; they will be his peoples, and God himself will be with them" (21:3).

John says that the city along with even its street was made of pure gold (21:18, 21), while the walls were fashioned from semiprecious jasper and the twelve gates from enormous pearls (21:18, 21). The description is magnificently bewildering—and John intends it to be that way, so that in our imagination we may be carried along with wonder at the splendor of all that God has prepared for his people. Some individuals have been offended by the material grandeur ascribed to the perfect city. John's description of the opulence of the New Jerusalem, however, is not a glorification of materialism, but rather a trivialization of all the materialism, all the opulence, that entrances the worldly-minded. Augustus could boast that he found Rome a city of brick and left it a city of marble (Suetonius, *Augustus* 28); all the wealth of human empires is as nothing compared to what God has prepared for those who love him. In a city in which gold bricks serve as paving stones, worldly wealth no longer has value or meaning; those who are promised a home in the former should liberate themselves from the lure of the latter.

John next turns his attention to aspects of life within this incredible city. The reader is no doubt surprised that he presents heaven without a temple. Unlike Ezekiel, who spends four chapters (40–43) in a detailed description of the new temple, John says, "I saw no temple in the city" (Revelation 21:22). There is no temple or sanctuary in the holy city, for the city itself is, once again, all sanctuary, all "Holy of Holies." The immediate presence of God is no longer in a reserved place, entered only by the high priest, and that but once a year; God is now accessible to all. The assurance that the city's "gates will never be shut by day" (21:25) conveys the sense of perfect freedom of access and fellowship with God. Normally the gates of ancient cities were closed during the night for security reasons, but the gates of this city do not need to be closed, for "there will be no night there" (21:25).

The angel shows John a sparkling river that flows crystal clear from the heavenly throne, which indicates its boundless supply (22:1). It was the hope of Israelite prophets that living waters would flow from Jerusalem in the age to come (Ezekiel 47:1-12; Zechariah 14:8), and the psalmist spoke of a "river whose streams make glad the city of God" (Psalm 46:4). Reminiscent of the garden of Eden (Genesis 2:9), the tree of life is present here, standing on either side of the river and yielding twelve kinds of fruit. Besides producing fruit to be eaten, the tree also has leaves that "are for the healing of the nations" (Revelation 22:2), sorely needed after human empires' ravaging of the nations. The saving benefits of the gospel promote the well-being of all aspects of personal and communal life.

Another link with the account in the opening chapters of Genesis is John's declaration that in the holy city there will no longer be anything accursed (22:3). After Adam and Eve had sinned by eating of the tree of knowledge, they were banished from Eden by the mercy of God lest they eat also of the tree of life and become immortal in their sin (Genesis 3:22-24). Now that redemption has been accomplished, it is safe to eat from the tree of life. Paradise lost is now paradise regained.

At this point the seer of Patmos directs the reader's attention to the most important feature of all: namely, that the throne of God and of the Lamb will be in the heavenly Jerusalem, and that God's servants "will worship him; they will see his face, and his name will be on their foreheads" (Revelation 22:3-4). Then the promise in Jesus' beatitude will be realized, namely, that "the pure in heart . . . will see God" (Matthew 5:8). But what does it mean to see God?

St. Augustine wrestled with this question in his classic work, *The City of God*. He asks whether, in heaven, when we close our eyelids, we will shut out the beatific vision. Very sensibly he concludes that this cannot be true, for to see God means more than to look at God, to gaze at God. In heaven, he says, "God will be seen by the eyes of the heart, which can see realities that are immaterial" (XXII.29). Here Augustine is reminding us that the verb "to see" also means to comprehend and understand. In its totality, then, one can say that to see God involves being near God, knowing God, and rejoicing in God all at the same time.

John's words, however, go beyond the thought of seeing God by either sensory or spiritual perception; he says that God's servants "will see his face" (Revelation 22:4). What special nuance of meaning does this expression convey? In antiquity to see the face of the king signified more than simply glancing up at the king when he might be riding by. The expression implied that one was granted an audience with the king and an opportunity to present one's petition in direct personal conversation (Genesis 43:3, 5; Exodus 10:28, 29; and elsewhere). Thus, to see God's face is not only to be in God's nearer presence but also to enjoy a relationship of absolute trust and openness. This is confirmed by John's following assertion, that God's "name will be on their foreheads," signifying their preciousness to God to whom they belong. In short, John is telling his readers that one day there will be granted to the servants of God that which had previously been the privilege of the heavenly creatures around God's throne (Revelation 4:2-11; see also Matthew 18:10). Or, in the words of the apostle Paul, "Now we see in a mirror, dimly, but then we will see face to face" (1 Corinthians 13:12). We are called to cultivate *here* the purity, the sanctification of our lives, that will prepare us for our encounter with the Holy One *there* (1 John 3:1-3; Hebrews 12:14).

The combination of purity with the vision of God not only is made in the Sermon on the Mount (Matthew 5:8) but is also reiterated more than once by early Christian writers. The author of the Letter to the Hebrews exhorts his readers to "pursue . . . holiness without which no one will see the Lord" (Hebrews 12:14). Though Christian believers are described as children of God, they are not yet what they will be hereafter, for when the Lord appears, "we will be like him, for we will see him as he is. And all who have this hope in him purify themselves, just as he is pure" (1 John 3:2-3).

EPILOGUE: CLOSING WARNINGS AND PROMISES

At first reading the concluding verses of Revelation appear to be a discordant assortment of brief, staccato-like warnings and promises. But more careful attention discloses the work of an artist who skillfully reiterates features that were introduced in the opening section of his book. Besides affirming the authenticity of his visionary experiences (22:6; 1:10-11), he characterizes his book as a genuine prophecy (22:7; 1:3), and indicates that it is to be read aloud in churches (22:18; 1:3). John claims for his work a threefold authentication: namely, God (22:6; 1:1), Christ (22:16; 1:1), and the angels who mediated it (22:16; 1:1).

In sharp contrast to Daniel, who was told to seal up the record of his visions "until the time of the end" (Daniel 12:4, 9), John is commanded, "Do not seal up the words of the prophecy of this book, for the time is near" (Revelation 22:10). In fact, the concluding verses reiterate four times (verses 6, 7, 12, 20) a theme found only three times in the rest of the book (1:1; 2:16; 3:11), namely, that Christ will come soon and that the interval before his return will be short. Because the time is short, there will be but little opportunity for repentance and change: the wicked are confirmed in their wickedness, the righteous in their righteousness (22:11; compare Daniel 12:10).

In the Christian doctrine of the last things, the imminence of the end is moral rather than chronological; each successive generation, so far as can be known to the contrary, may be the last generation. In that sense, the time is always near (22:10). It is therefore the part of wisdom for believers to be ready to meet their Lord. And while Christ's coming may tarry beyond our own lifetime, our own encounter with Christ before his judgment seat is never further away for us than the end of our earthly life.

The last two of the seven beatitudes in Revelation pronounce a blessing upon those who obey the prophetic message contained in the book (22:7), and upon those who wash (present tense) their robes (22:14). The washing of one's robes is connected with the sacrifice of Christ (7:14); it is not a matter of self-reformation but the saving and purifying effect of identifying with Jesus' death and preserving that loyalty intact through the rest of our lives. It is these who "will have the right to the tree of life and may enter the city by the gates" (22:14). Jesus identifies himself here with the same words God had used at the outset of the book, and here we come near the roots of the later doctrine of the Trinity: both the Father *and* the Son are simultaneously "the Alpha and the Omega, the first and the last, the beginning and the end" (1:8; 22:13).

The privilege of entrance is heightened by listing those who are excluded: "Outside are the dogs and sorcerers and fornicators and murderers and idolaters, and everyone who loves and practices falsehood" (22:15). "Outside" does not mean that they are in close proximity to the city; for the idea of "outside" we should compare Jesus' reference to "the outer darkness" (Matthew 8:12). This list of those who are excluded resembles in some respects the earlier list of those consigned to the lake of fire (21:8). These lists clearly characterize those in league with Rome and its violence and idolatry, but they also serve as warnings to John's congregations not to prove cowardly or to agree with the lies around them for expediency's sake.

When books were copied by hand, scribes would occasionally add comments of their own or leave out words they thought were unsuitable. John therefore includes at the end of his book a solemn warning (similar to that found in Deuteronomy 4:2; 12:32) declaring that nothing should be added or deleted, for the very good reason that it is a revelation from God (Revelation 22:18-19). Like the open scroll that John himself was told to swallow in its entirety (10:9-10), Revelation must be heard, wrestled with, and "kept" as a whole—both those parts that are sweet in our mouths and those that leave a feeling of bitterness in our stomach.

* * * * * * * *

The Book of Revelation provided pastoral encouragement for Christians who were confronted with persecution and cruelty and pastoral warning for Christians tempted to seek the profits of partnership with a seductively powerful system. The book was written, we know, to enable them to control their fear, to renew their commitment, to resist temptations, and to sustain their vision. John's final sentence is a benediction: "The grace of the Lord Jesus be with all the saints. Amen" (22:21). Thus, the concluding note is one of comfort, of love, of encouragement. There could be no more fitting end for a book that contains horrible visions of great monsters and catastrophic judgments. John closes his book with visions of hope and of heaven, promising that at the last we shall enjoy the vision of God because of the grace of the Lord Jesus Christ.

FOR FURTHER READING

In addition to consulting articles in Bible dictionaries concerning John, Patmos, Ephesus, Smyrna, Antipas, Nicolaitans, and other names that occur in the Book of Revelation, the following will be of assistance in further study:

Barclay, William. *The Revelation of John.* 2 vols. Philadelphia: Westminster Press, 1959 (231 and 297 pages). A useful, if dated, commentary designed primarily for laypeople.

Carey, Greg. *Ultimate Things: An Introduction to Jewish and Christian Apocalyptic Literature.* St. Louis: Chalice Press, 2005 (304 pages). An excellent introduction to the genre of "apocalypse" and to the body of literature that falls within this genre.

deSilva, David A. *AR271 The Seven Cities of Revelation.* Logos Mobile Education. Bellingham, WA: Lexham Press, 2018. A video course introducing the life contexts of each of the seven cities through attention to their archaeology and artifacts and featuring over two hundred photos taken on location.

deSilva, David A. *Unholy Allegiances: Heeding Revelation's Warning.* Peabody, MA: Hendrickson, 2013 (132 pages). An immersion into the archaeological, ideological, and historical setting of the seven churches, the challenge of Revelation within that setting, and Revelation's ongoing challenge to contemporary Christians.

Howard-Brook, Wes and Anthony Gwyther. *Unveiling Empire: Reading Revelation Then and Now.* New York: Orbis, 1999 (343 pages). A provocative reading of Revelation as an indictment of ancient and modern political and economic domination systems.

Keener, Craig S. *Revelation.* The NIV Application Commentary. Grand Rapids: Zondervan, 2000 (575 pages). An accessible commentary particularly rich in suggestions for how the word of Revelation continues to speak to contemporary communities of faith.

Koester, Craig R. *Revelation.* Yale Anchor Bible. New Haven: Yale University Press, 2014 (881 pages). A richly informed critical commentary written by a meticulous scholar.

Kraybill, J. Nelson. *Apocalypse and Allegiance: Worship, Politics, and Devotion in the Book of Revelation.* Grand Rapids, MI: Brazos Press, 2010 (224 pages). An excellent introduction to the Roman imperial context of Revelation, particular in its political and economic aspects.

Reddish, Mitchell G. *Revelation.* Smyth & Helwys Bible Commentary. Macon, GA: Smyth & Helwys, 2001. An accessible commentary particularly rich in connections with the rest of the scriptural canon, Christian theology, and the ongoing life of the church.

Rowland, Christopher C. "The Book of Revelation: Introduction, Commentary, and Reflections," vol. XII *The New Interpreter's Bible.* Nashville: Abingdon Press, 1998 (243 pages). An accessible commentary by a renowned scholar of apocalyptic literature.

Schüssler Fiorenza, Elisabeth. *Revelation: Vision of a Just World.* Minneapolis: Fortress Press, 1991 (150 pages). An assessment of Revelation in terms of liberation and feminist theology.

Wilson, Mark. *Revelation.* Zondervan Illustrated Bible Backgrounds Commentary. Grand Rapids: Zondervan, 2007 (142 pages). A lavishly illustrated introduction to the archaeological, geographical, and cultural world of Roman Asia Minor and reading Revelation in its historical context.

Witherington, Ben, III. *Revelation.* Cambridge: Cambridge University Press, 2003 (307 pages). An accessible commentary on Revelation by a leading New Testament scholar.

For discussion of the millennium and chapter 20 of Revelation, see the books mentioned in note #2 under the Chapter 11 heading on page 144.

NOTES

Chapter 1:
Introducing the Book of Revelation

1   Reported by Eusebius in his *Church History* V. xxv. 7.

2   His Letter to the Philippians, *11.3*.

3   An English translation of these and other apocalyptic
    books is available in *The Old Testament Pseudepigrapha*,
    vol. I, *Apocalyptic Literature and Testaments*, ed. James H.
    Charlesworth (Garden City, NY: Doubleday, 1983).

4   John is fond of sevens; he mentions seven golden lampstands,
    seven stars, seven flaming torches, seven spirits of God, seven
    eyes, seven seals, seven angels, seven trumpets, seven thunders,
    seven heads on the dragon, seven plagues, seven bowls, seven
    mountains, and seven kings. Furthermore, without directly
    enumerating them, John includes seven beatitudes scattered
    throughout his book (see note #1 under the Chapter 2 heading
    on page 142) as well as the sevenfold praise presented to the
    Lamb (5:12).

Chapter 2:
John's Vision of the Heavenly Christ

1   There are seven beatitudes scattered through the Book of
     Revelation. The other six are at 14:13; 16:15; 19:9; 20:6; 22:7, 14.

2   Ignatius of Antioch writes to well-established churches in
     Tralles and Magnesia in about AD 110; it is likely, then, that
     congregations existed in these cities as well by the time John
     wrote Revelation. He incidentally also writes letters to the
     congregations in Ephesus, Smyrna, and Philadelphia, providing
     informative windows into the ongoing lives of the Christians
     there.

3   See also Testament of Levi 3.4-6; 1 Enoch 20:7 (some manu-
     scripts of which enumerate the archangels at six, others at
     seven).

4   Whether the seer had writing materials on Patmos and was able
     to write the book while in exile or whether this could be done
     only after the death of Domitian (AD 96) when John returned
     once again to Ephesus is not known.

5   Against the caricatures of church history produced by such a
     reading, see further D. A. deSilva, *Unholy Allegiances: Heeding
     Revelation's Warning* (Peabody: Hendrickson, 2013), 103–104.

6   The rendering "candlesticks" in some English versions is a
     mistake in translation; candles were not invented until the
     Middle Ages.

Chapter 3:
Prophetic Words to the Churches

1   On the "works of the Nicolaitans" (2:6), see the section in this
     book titled "The Oracle to the Church in Pergamum" on
     page 43.

2   As recorded in the Thanksgiving Scroll (1QH 2:22) and the War

Scroll (1QM 4:9). In Revelation 2:9 John may also be objecting to his fellow Jews' willingness to buy toleration from the empire at the price, imposed since AD 70, of giving to the chief god of the Roman pantheon (whom John would identify with Satan, the chief demon) the tribute that had formerly been given to the support and upkeep of the Jerusalem temple. See deSilva, *Unholy Allegiances*, 87–88.

Chapter 5:
John's Vision of God and the Lamb

1   See "A Service of Word and Table IV," *The United Methodist Hymnal* (Nashville: The United Methodist Publishing House, 1989), 28.

Chapter 6:
Opening the Seven Seals of God's Scroll

1   The tribe of Dan is not mentioned, perhaps because of the tradition that the Antichrist would arise from this tribe. The tradition may have had its source in Genesis 49:17 (compare the omission of the same tribe from 1 Chronicles 4–7). The total of twelve tribes is maintained by replacing the name of Joseph with the names of his two sons, Ephraim and Manasseh.

Chapter 8:
The Satanic Counterfeit: The Dragon and the Two Beasts

1   It is not really proper to speak of a doctrine of the "Trinity" in the first century AD: the early Christian recognition of the divinity of God, Christ, and the Holy Spirit is not *yet* a belief in a "Trinity" as would be expressed in the creeds and councils of the fourth century. However, it does seem that the dragon and two beasts represent a counterfeit corresponding to God, Christ, and the Holy Spirit.

2   In the Hebrew alphabet (which consists of consonants only), the
      tenth letter has the numerical value of 10, but the eleventh letter
      represents 20, and the following letters carry on by tens until
      100. Thereafter, the letters carry on by hundreds (200, and so
      on). Thus, the "full" spelling of "Nero Caesar" in Hebrew letters
      is N, R, W, N, Q, S, R. These letters have the following numerical
      values: N = 50, R = 200, W = 6, N = 50, Q = 100, S = 60, and
      R = 200. The emperor's name was typically written *Neron* in
      Greek and *Nero* in Latin, hence the variant spellings and sums.

Chapter 11:
The Final Victory and the Last Judgment

1   The word *Hallelujah* transliterates a Hebrew expression that
      means "Praise Jah," that is, "Praise the Lord." It occurs only here
      in the New Testament (19:1, 3, 4, and 6).

2   For discussions of what can be said for and against each of the
      main views of the millennium, see Robert G. Clouse, ed., *The
      Meaning of the Millennium: Four Views* (Downers Grove, IL:
      InterVarsity Press, 1977) and Darrell L. Bock, ed., *Three Views
      on the Millennium and Beyond* (Grand Rapids: Zondervan,
      1999); and for a comprehensive discussion of the history of
      the interpretation of Revelation, see Arthur W. Wainwright,
      Mysterious Apocalypse: Interpreting the Book of Revelation
      (Nashville: Abingdon Press, 1993).

3   See, for example, Jubilees 30:21-23; 1 Enoch 47.3, 81.1-4;
      Martyrdom of Isaiah 9.22.

4   In the King James Version it occurs also at 22:19, but here all the
      best manuscript evidence reads "tree of life."